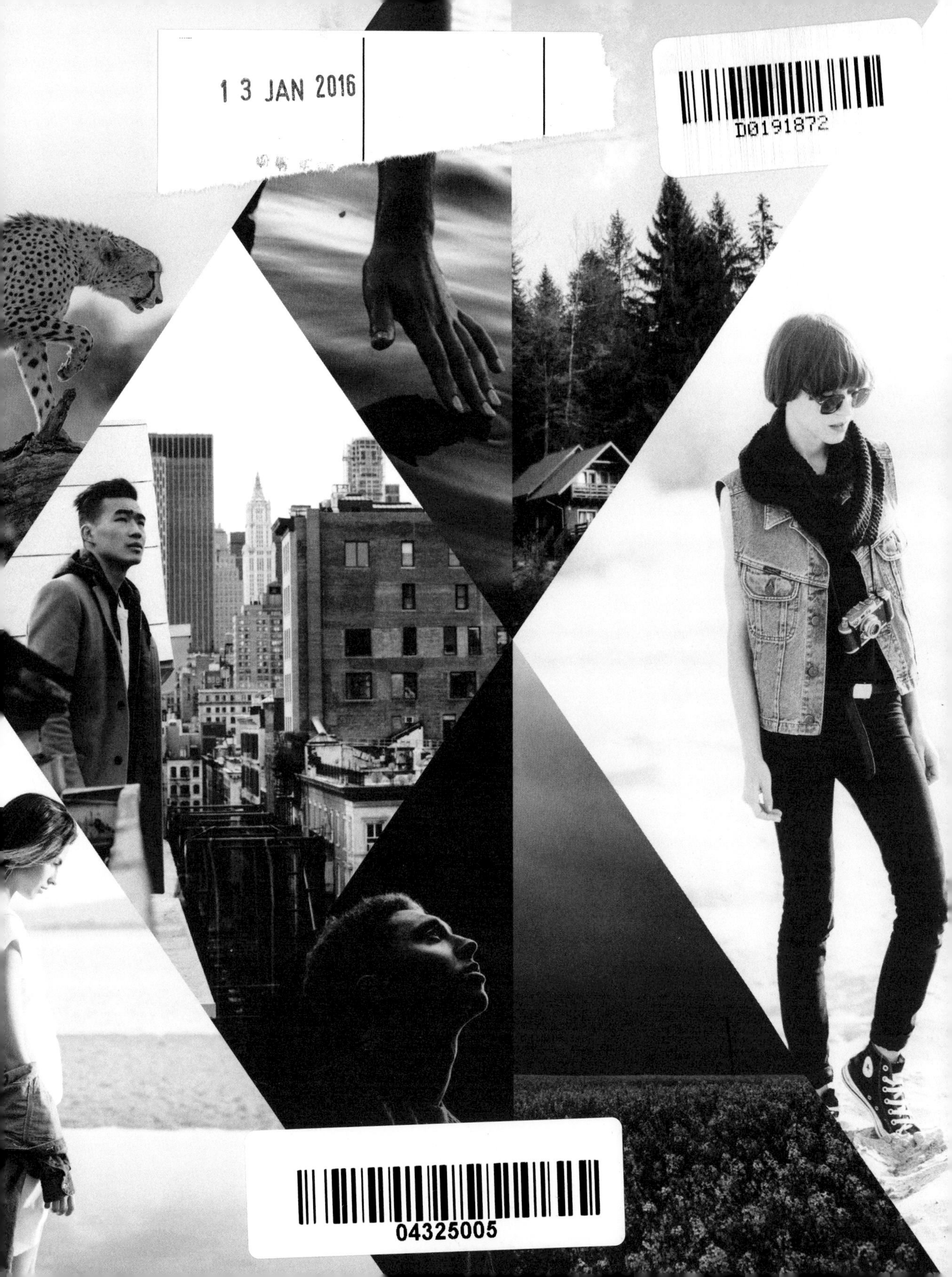

Published in Nashville, Tennessee, by Thomas Nelson. Thomas Nelson is a registered trademark of HarperCollins Christian Publishing.

Thomas Nelson, Inc., titles may be purchased in bulk for educational, business, fund-raising, or sales promotional use. For information, please e-mail SpecialMarkets@ ThomasNelson.com.

The Voice™ translation © 2012 Ecclesia Bible Society

All rights reserved.

Library of Congress Cataloging-in-Publication Data

[ISBN-9780718036942]

Printed in the United States of America

15 14 13 12 11 WOR 5 4 3 2 1

THOMAS NELSON
Since 1798

NASHVILLE   MEXICO CITY   RIO DE JANEIRO

ABRUPT MEDIA

THE ✝ ONE

EXPERIENCE JESUS

CARLOS DARBY

JUDAH SMITH   CHARLOTTE GAMBILL   GARY CLARKE   CARL LENTZ

CONTENTS

"Let *the good news*, the story you have heard from the beginning of your journey, live in *and take hold of* you. If that happens *and you focus on the good news*, then you will always remain in a relationship with the Son and the Father. This is what He promised us: eternal life."

1 JOHN 2:24

EXPERIENCE JESUS

The One: Experience Jesus is centered on illuminating the Scriptures for a generation that speaks in a visual language. It's about making the Scriptures and the themes found in the Bible more approachable and less intimidating. We're living in a visual time; the ways in which people engage and respond to content are rapidly changing, and methods of communicating a message are becoming more aesthetic.

Every picture gives us a glimpse of a unique life. Images capture moments and allow us to relive the experiences again in our minds. Sometimes these images are so powerful that they can shape culture, rallying people to act and make a stand for good. Sometimes they remind us of events in history we regret. They can also help us learn.

Psychologist Jerome Bruner of New York University says that people only remember 10 percent of what they hear and 20 percent of what they read, but about 80 percent of what they see and do.[1] Jesus taught people about His kingdom using parables to illustrate a message. I imagine that they would create these stories in their minds, see the ways of God's kingdom, and be able to apply it to their own lives.

This visual book is here to serve you in learning more about the power of the gospel—the good news of the relationship that we have access to—and to provide a means of triggering your memory. The images ensure that the information will stick with you in everyday life.

"Every picture gives us a glimpse of a unique life. Images capture moments and allow us to relive the experiences again in our minds."

---

[1] "Power of Visual Communication," http://www.slideshare.net/NounProject/the-power-of-visual-communication.

The scriptures you'll see in the book have been taken from *The Voice*, a powerful and illustrative translation of the Bible that perfectly complements the visual aspects of *The One*. We believe the visuals and Bible translation together will engage the next generation of Bible readers and present the themes of the book in a way that will draw people in and bring enhanced understanding and recollection of the content of the book. Ultimately, readers will experience lasting change to their lives.

There are so many stereotypical images attached to the Scriptures. Although these are historically relevant, they don't speak to us the way more current images do. To keep future generations engaged with the Scriptures, we need to allow individuals to express their own unique style as they follow Jesus. Images in *The One* have been created in a variety of locations around the world and with people of many cultures. Our goal is to point to the fact that Jesus calls us all, today, wherever we are and however we look. He looks at the heart.

The Chapters

In the first part of this book, we look at the overall context for our relationship with God. Through the story of Adam and Eve, we see the rise and fall of His intended relationship with us. Abraham then shows us that a relationship with God isn't based on works, but is only through faith. Finally, the salvation plan from Genesis is played out in the New Testament; our Savior is here and is dealing with separation through sin and death for good and gives us the Holy Spirit to remain with us always.

The second part of the book looks at what we can learn from the relationship Jesus had with His Father and what it means to be His follower and a disciple today. We end on the most important part of making our walk with Jesus something that is real and to be experienced: the mystery revealed.

The personal stories shared, the interviews conducted, and the features written all point to the power of the good news that Jesus came to give us. We now have access to the most amazing relationship we could imagine with our living God. This is indeed good news, because it's free, it's available to all, and it's worth more than anything else.

It's the mystery revealed: Jesus lives in each and every one of those who accept His message, and He's calling those who have not yet experienced the relationship.

Through this visual book, I hope that your faith is stirred as you engage with the contemplation sections and that you raise your expectations about what a life with Jesus means. The book is not about adding more to your daily to-do list, but taking away clutter and changing perspectives, bringing you closer to Jesus. I pray that you'll come away with a greater sense of value and confidence so that you can share Him with your world and experience Him in a whole new way, because the gospel has captured your heart.

— *Carlos Darby*

THE RISE & FALL

The beginning of humanity's sin begins with a tree
and ends with a tree; first, the tree of knowledge of
good and evil; and finally, the cross on which Jesus
dies. The first tree offers fruit that leads to death, but
the second offers a death that leads to eternal life.

Photographers: Adam & Eve: Hannah Radley-Bennett
Landscape: Ed Peers / Animals: Marlon Du Toit

GOD: LET THERE BE LIGHT.

And light flashed into being. God saw that the light was
beautiful and good, and He separated the light from the
darkness. God named the light "day" and darkness
"night." Evening gave way to morning. That was day one.

GENESIS 1:3–5

GOD: EARTH, GENERATE LIFE!

Produce a vast variety of living creatures—
domesticated animals, *small* creeping creatures,
and wild animals that roam the earth.

GENESIS 1:24

SO GOD DID *JUST THAT*

He created humanity in His image, created them male and female.
Then God blessed them and gave them *this directive*: "Be fruitful
and multiply. Populate the earth. *I make you trustees of My estate*,
so care for My creation and rule over the fish of the sea, the birds
of the sky, and every creature that roams across the earth."

GENESIS 1:27–28

THE WOMAN *APPROACHED THE TREE,*

eyed its fruit, and coveted its *mouth-watering, wisdom-granting* beauty. She plucked a fruit from the tree and ate. She then offered *the fruit* to her husband who was close by, and he ate as well.

GENESIS 3:6

SO THE ETERNAL GOD BANISHED

Adam *and Eve* from the garden
of Eden *and exiled humanity from
paradise, sentencing humans to laborious lives*
working the very ground man came from.

GENESIS 3:23

IF ONE MAN'S SIN

brought a reign of death—*that's Adam's legacy*—how much more will those who receive grace in abundance and the free gift of redeeming justice reign in life by means of one other man—Jesus the Anointed.

ROMANS 5:17

THROUGH HIS EYES

———

God chose us to be in a relationship with Him even before He laid out plans for this world; He wanted us to live holy lives characterized by love, *free from sin*, and blameless before Him. He destined us to be adopted as His children through *the covenant* Jesus the Anointed *inaugurated in His sacrificial life*. This was His pleasure and His will *for us*.

EPHESIANS 1:4–5

Words: Carlos Darby / Photography: Hannah Radley-Bennett
Styling: Sharna-Marie Francis

C hildren are brought into the world under so many different circumstances, and while some of those are unplanned by the parents, we are never unplanned by God.

I was an unexpected arrival and never saw my biological father past the age of three, but that didn't stop me from seeing God move in powerful ways throughout my life. Over the years, I have learned to keep things simple so that with childlike faith I could see my experience of Jesus as a genuine family relationship.

I married my wife, Katie, in 2009, and a few years later we planned to have our first baby, who was followed by another two years later. We knew it wouldn't always be perfect, but we had children because we wanted to enjoy them, love them, and share our lives with them. The love we have for them is greater than I ever expected, and we want them to know we're always there for them and will always love them. If they started saying things like, "Look! I tidied my bedroom. You must really love me now," then as parents we would know to question how we had communicated our love for them.

As children of God, we need to know that His love for us is perfect, complete, and unchanging. Too often we can reduce our relationship with Him to a business contract we entered into when we decided to follow Him, one governed by regulations and performance targets. Or we can behave as though we are a burden to God, an unexpected arrival that He doesn't quite know what to do with.

But God planned us and He chose us. Our story with Him began long ago.

The Whole Story

I love going to the movie theater and watching epic films. But imagine if you're going to watch the latest blockbuster, and you arrive an hour late. You sit down to watch and have to try to figure out the characters, their motives, and the storyline, all on your own. It would be confusing, and you might have a general idea about the plot by the end of the film, but the experience would be less impactful and there would be elements of the film you never understood or just missed out on altogether.

For many people, the story of creation can seem irrelevant. But in essence, creation is the beginning of our movie.

We discount the Old Testament as a collection of historical stories that became obsolete when Jesus came, and think ourselves fortunate not to have to sacrifice animals and climb mountains to speak to God. But the God of the Old Testament is the same God of today. Understanding where our relationship with Him began can

"Too often we can reduce our relationship with Him to a business contract we entered into when we decided to follow Him, one governed by regulations and performance targets."

help us grasp who we are, who He is, and what the good news of the gospel really means.

When we look from Genesis to Revelation, we see Jesus and God's plan for humanity at every step. Looking at the beginning of the story shows us the deeper truths about God's intended relationship with us and why there is a need for reconciliation between God and humanity. Through the key characters and their motivations, we can better understand the importance of what we see unfold through to the end of the New Testament. How we see the beginning of the story will impact our perception of Jesus and therefore our experience of a life following Him.

In any epic story, the beginning has to be powerful. In Genesis, we see God as the creator of all things, but we are also shown God's heart. He was creating out of a desire to establish an environment for us where we would be the focus of His love. He didn't create to impress Himself or us; He didn't create because He was bored and thought He'd play *SimCity*. He planned everything for a purpose, that we might experience Him and His creativity.

As seen in Romans, God has used His creation to show us who He is—all we have to do is look around to see Him.

> From the beginning, creation in its magnificence enlightens us to His nature. Creation itself makes His undying power and divine identity clear, even though they are invisible; and it voids the excuses *and ignorant claims* of these people. (Rom. 1:20)

God shouldn't have to prove Himself to us any further, but as we know, our humanity leads us to question everything. When God created His first children, Adam and Eve, He knew beforehand what they would do—yet He created them anyway, and He created them with the ability to choose. You *do* have to ask yourself, "Why bother?" The Bible tells us that God's central motivation is love, He is love, and everything He does comes out of

"When love has let us down in the past, we need to experience His love for ourselves."

that. Not a Hollywood love, but an unconditional, selfless kind of love that is based on choice.

Anyone who does not love does not know God, because God is love. (1 John 4:8)

Choice is an important aspect of creation because God chose to create everything; Adam and Eve chose to disobey their God. God gave us the ability to choose, because to be in a relationship based on love, there has to be the option or it isn't really love. God could have forced us to love Him, but that's a contradiction in terms. Love has to be freely given, received, and returned.

Adam and Eve were given every good thing they needed but interpreted His withholding of something they wanted as a lack of love— how often do we do the same today? In our humanity, we perceive God as someone who withholds for no good reason.

Our finite minds can't comprehend His infiniteness, so we live by our own rules and regulations, choose our own paths, eat our own forbidden fruit, and question the love and plan of God when things don't work out the way we wanted. Or worse still: if things *do* work out the way we want, we remove God from the picture because, just as Adam and Eve were trying to do, we have elevated ourselves to be like God so that we no longer need Him at all.

Choice is something that was also given to the angels. They too were created by God and were given the honor of experiencing God in heaven and being in His presence. As head musician in heaven, Satan became jealous of the power and glory of God and wanted it for himself. He was thrown out of heaven along with one-third of all the angels. This master of lies now works on earth, passing on his own misconceptions about God onto humanity.

Starting with Adam and Eve, we see the same story play out as the one we saw with Satan. We can question God's love and authority, desire to be the ones in control, and separate ourselves from God's love. The difference now is that we have a way back.

How we choose to love God and to be loved by God is the foundation of our relationship with Him. We can use all our own efforts to become like God in our own strength, or we can use His strength to become more like Jesus.

I don't want to take for granted this amazing privilege to be called a child of God. So I choose Jesus.

For Jesus is not some high priest who has no sympathy for our weaknesses *and flaws*. He has already been tested in every way that we are tested; but He emerged victorious, without failing God. So let us step boldly to the throne of grace, where we can find mercy and grace to help when we need it most. (Heb. 4:15–16)

Love, Honor, Gratitude

Everyone loves a good romance flick (occasionally). Unrequited love is a big theme in these films, and we all know the formula. Girl longs for the love of the bad boy, dreaming of their life together. She has her heart broken, sharing her pain with a friend who has always loved her in secret. He hopes that one day she will stop focusing on something that isn't real and see that he can offer her true and lasting love. *Ahh*.

The Bible is also a love story—one of God longing to bring humanity back into the right relationship with Him. Sometimes, though, we make God out to be the ignored suitor in a teenage love triangle, desperate for our attention, affection, and time as He tries to lead us away from the path that results in heartbreak. God does love us, and people need to hear that, but He is also God. He is sovereign, He created us, and He sacrificed His only Son because of the love He has for humanity. The honor is all ours.

We all want intimacy with God and have a space in our hearts that can only be filled by Jesus. But *love* is a word that is used in so many contexts, on so many levels. Our past experiences form our perspectives about what *love* means, and when we are told that God is love, we come to that with our own misconceptions. When love has let us down in the past, we need to experience His love for ourselves. Once we receive Jesus, we become spiritually alive, and as the Bible says, we will be able to please God in the only way possible: through our faith that we are His and He is ours. We get to be friends and children of God. Once we understand that, we can go out and be His hands and feet to bring unconditional love to others.

"Gratitude bestows reverence, allowing us to encounter everyday epiphanies, those transcendent moments of awe that change forever how we experience life and the world."
— John Milton

This great quote by John Milton reminds me of a simple yet vital key to experiencing Jesus: gratitude. No matter the circumstances I face, or how difficult it is to see the bigger picture of God's plan, God is love and He cares about my life. My personal story is part of the love story that started back in Genesis, when God took a huge risk in creating us, but one that was in His eyes totally worth the sacrifices He had to make.

This is not a love we can see through the eyes of any film script or past experience. We can only see it clearly through Jesus.

He is the embodiment of our peace, *sent once and for all* to take down the great barrier of hatred and hostility that has divided us so that we can be one. He offered His body *on the sacrificial altar* to bring an end to the law's ordinances and dictations *that separated Jews from the outside nations. His desire was* to create in His body one new humanity from the two *opposing groups*, thus creating peace. (Eph. 2:14–15)

Carlos Darby

———

Carlos is from a Colombian background, was raised in the United Kingdom, and now lives in the south of Spain with his wife, Katie, and their two little girls, Maya and India. Carlos started Abrupt Media with Katie, after years of working on publications and developing concepts to illuminate the scriptures for a visual generation.

Connect with Carlos on IG @carlos_abruptmedia

GOLD IN THE GARBAGE

LOCATION: NEW YORK CITY, USA

Words: Anny / Photography: Evan Rummel

When I arrived to meet Steve D'Agrosa, he apologized in advance for being somewhat distracted by preparations for Friday Night Live, the weekly church hangout. His distraction betrayed the passion he embodied and the commitment he dedicated to his church. He placed his phone to one side so he could give me his undivided attention and explained that in no uncertain terms was this always the case.

Steve's story begins in Queens, New York City, where he attended Catholic private schools throughout his childhood. Although it wasn't always openly expressed, he knew that he was loved by his family; however, things were very different at school.

"I was really overweight as a kid and I got picked on and bullied because of it," he recalled. "There were the cool kids, and then there was us, the horrible kids."

He had to deal with the hurt by himself. "I love my parents, but being old-school Italian, their mentality was, 'You're a man—don't cry about it, don't talk about it, just fight back,'" he explains. "But how do you fight back against ten kids making fun of you?"

As time progressed, Steve didn't have to fight back.

"I was twelve or thirteen when some of the kids invited me to a birthday party," he said. "Everyone was smoking weed and all of a sudden I had an option: I could say no and keep getting terrorized, or smoke weed and start hanging out with them. That's the moment when I made the decision to out-smoke them, out-drink them, and out-party them everywhere we went. I finally had the chance to be accepted."

That was the start of a long and painful downward spiral for Steve. Except it didn't feel like that at first. He smoked weed daily, and at fourteen, he took his first ecstasy pill. He said, "I loved it. It was amazing. I was high as a kite. I did that every weekend for a while, then that quickly became every couple of days. When you're on ecstasy, you don't really function, so somebody once gave me cocaine to bring me down. Little did I know that it would snowball into what it did."

By high school, Steve was selling drugs to his friends to feed a habit that by this point was costing him hundreds of dollars a week. He went on to college, where he continued to sell drugs.

"I was making thousands of dollars in a weekend and rolling in money," Steve said. "It was girls, drugs, and parties seven days a week."

"Every couple of days I'd pawn four to five hundred dollars' worth of stuff. Because of me, they no longer own any gold; I even sold my dad's wedding ring."

Steve dabbled with Vicodin during high school, a drug that he tells me is like heroin and is very addictive. By the time he reached the age of twenty-one, dabbling had turned into daily usage and the cost was killing him financially.

"Rather than getting help to break the addiction, I was looking for a cheaper way to carry on feeding it," he explained. "Somebody introduced me to heroin, and I started doing that. This was the turning point when the party and drug scene went from awesome to miserable. The addiction to heroin is another level. It's unbelievable what it does to you; it consumes your life."

By the age of twenty-six, he was spending between four and five hundred dollars' on heroin each day—much more than he was selling. Every penny he made was spent on drugs.

"If I made two thousand dollars, within two or three days, I was broke," he said. Eventually, he had to think of other ways to make money. "One of the ways was selling my family's jewelry," Steve admitted. "I stole it, and every couple of days I'd pawn four to five hundred dollars' worth of stuff. Because of me, they no longer own any gold; I even sold my dad's wedding ring."

He was, however, thrown a lifeline when he was hired as a handyman at a multimillion-dollar property overlooking the ocean. It was an opportunity to get back on his feet, but as a heroin addict, it was also an opportunity to get money to buy drugs.

"One day, I snooped around the house while they were out and found their jewelry stash. I stole approximately one hundred thirty-five thousand dollars' worth of jewelry and pawned it at the pawnshop down the block. I wasn't even slick about it and used my own ID—genius! I wasn't thinking; I was just looking for the next fix."

Steve was subsequently arrested for robbery and put in jail. Although jail was a terrible experience, he felt that he belonged there.

He said, "I related to everybody there, so with the exception of the handcuffs and the bars, it was exactly where I'd been living on the outside. I was still a heroin addict and could buy it in jail. It was dirty. People were bleeding, being sick, and going through withdrawals. It's hell without the heat."

Steve's uncle bailed him out of jail, but with nowhere else to go and a restraining order preventing him from returning to collect any of his belongings, he went back to stay at his parents' house.

"I was in my old bedroom, sleeping on two couch cushions and a couple of towels on the floor. My parents locked the bedrooms, so I was literally like a crackhead—living on the floor, eating on the floor. It was horrible."

After three days of this, Steve knew that he'd reached a breaking point.

"I grew up as a Catholic so I had a crucifix in my room, and that night I was contemplating whether to kill myself. I was causing everyone so much pain, besides what I was doing to myself. I knew my parents would be upset, but I believed that it'd be best for everybody and a relief for them."

Sitting on the ground and looking at that crucifix, Steve made a conscious decision to take his own life.

At that moment, for some reason, his friend Alex popped into his mind.

"I grew up with him but hadn't spoken to him since I screwed him over seven years earlier. I knew he was a Christian guy, so I figured that if anyone could talk me off the edge it would be him. I sent him a message that said, 'Do you have a pastor who can call me? I just need someone to talk to.' He emailed me right back and told me that he went to a church in London, and they'd just started in New York, so I should check it out."

Steve wasn't interested in going to a Christian church, full of weird and judgmental people and a pastor pointing and yelling at them. However, that message provided a significant turning point in his life.

"When I contacted my friend Alex, it was the moment when I made the decision to at least try to fix this," he revealed.

Steve went to Narcotics Anonymous, but he didn't find any answers there.

"One thing that stood out was how miserable everybody was. They were telling us that we were going to be stuck with this for the rest of our lives, so we just had to deal with it. I wanted to know how to break it, but they couldn't tell me."

He decided to look into the Muslim and Jewish faiths and how other people had broken free of drug addiction. "I typed: 'Muslim man gets delivered from drugs' and 'Jewish man gets delivered from drugs' into YouTube, and the caption at the bottom of both videos said: 'When he meets Jesus.'"

Alex's words rang in Steve's mind. "I didn't want anything to do with the church, but I trusted Alex and his opinion. He'd guaranteed that I'd walk out of there different, and that's all I needed to know. I thought, if I can walk in somewhere and walk out different, then I'm game. Let's go!"

Pulling up outside a club at 9:20 p.m. to go to church was understandably confusing for Steve.

"I'd been to [places like these] high on drugs and I had to make sure that it was actually church and I wasn't going back to a club night," he explained. Standing in line, he had a change of heart and decided to leave. "I was getting ready to walk away when a girl from the church's connect team walked up to me and started talking. I didn't know who she was and assumed that she was trying to cut in the line.

"She asked how long I'd been coming, and when I told her it was my first time, she asked if I was a Christian. I started balling my eyes out! I hadn't noticed that the line had been moving as we were talking, so I found myself walking into Gramercy [the church venue]. It was almost like God put her there to block me from leaving and get me inside."

Then, as if she were part of a tag team, another host approached him. "I wasn't used to rules, so I didn't know where to stand and was afraid I was going to mess it up," Steve said.

When she heard that Steve had no idea what he was doing or what was going on, she gave him a huge hug. "That was the first hug that I had been given in years, so immediately I felt that something was different here," he said.

She seated him near the front, and he cried for most of the service.

"I thought it was amazing and left feeling good, but I wasn't saved. I was still on my meds and went home to email Alex. I told him it had been awesome, but there were seven services so I was going to give it another shot next week and see which one I liked the best."

Steve arrived at 7:30 a.m. the next Sunday, even before the gates were up at Gramercy.

"I was first in line and waited," he said. "I met a couple of people, I went inside, I sat down, and I sat there all day long. The pastor, Carl, was preaching a message called 'Gold in the Garbage.'"

During the salvation call, Steve admits that he wasn't going to raise his hand, but that changed.

"Carl said, 'Raise your hand if you want Jesus, bearing in mind that God is not interested in whether or not you're qualified—He just wants to use you because you're available,'" Steve recalled. "Immediately I thought, *Well, I'm not qualified for anything. I'm available and I've got no job right now, so I can do whatever you need,* and I raised my hand. That's when I got saved."

Steve stayed all day for every service, raising his hand for every salvation call and listening to Pastor Carl's message over and over again. By the 9:30 p.m. service, Steve was worshipping with his hands held high. The message spoke to him so much that he was convinced Alex had called Pastor Carl.

"I was convinced that Carl wrote it around my life and was talking about me, so I wanted to thank him and let him know that I appreciated it."

As he walked to his car after service, Pastor Carl came through the back door of Gramercy.

"I told him I'd been asking people if I could meet him and that the message he wrote was for me. Then I asked him if he knew my friend Alex. I can only imagine what he was thinking, because he just stood there looking at me, then stopped me in my tracks to ask my name."

Steve wanted to know what he was supposed to do next, and Pastor Carl's advice was simple: he told him to just keep showing up.

"He gave me a hug and said, 'Hey, man, welcome home.' That resonated with me, because for the last fifteen years, I hadn't been welcomed anywhere."

It's been three years and Steve hasn't used heroin since that day and he hasn't had to take any more medication for depression. Although his doctor warned him against it, Steve flushed all of his pills.

"I told [my doctor] that I'd walked into this church and didn't feel like I needed to take them anymore. He reminded me that I had a major addiction, and if I stopped the medication, then my heart would stop."

What actually happened was that the addiction miraculously disappeared.

"I felt normal," Steve recalled. "Sleeping at night, waking up in the morning; no stomach cramps, no nausea, no withdrawal symptoms at all. Don't get me wrong—God had a lot of work to do in me as a human being, but as far as the addiction [was concerned], it was gone."

"I really consumed myself with Jesus. I wasn't working, so for five months I watched sermons on TV, went to four connect groups, read my Bible, listened to worship music, and went to church on Wednesdays and Sundays. God took away the addiction, but then surrounded me with people who helped teach me how to be a human being and not continue thinking and behaving like an addict."

Given his past, Steve says it is surprising that he is even alive today.

"My life has always been a scandal, but now I'm a scandal for the house [of God]. I shouldn't be here, we shouldn't be talking, I shouldn't be doing a photo shoot, I shouldn't be in church. I should be in a crack house somewhere, or dead.

"I made a conscious decision to go at it, and I know I'll upset a lot of people. My ten-year plan is to have a target on my back for Christians and non-Christians alike—people coming at me for good and for bad. I want to have to walk around with security, not because of who I am but because of what I'm doing. Knowing that I need it only because people want to take me out—I want that. That's what I seek: to be kicking in the doors of crack houses. That was normal life for me five years ago, so why wouldn't I do that for Jesus now?"

Steve is completely sold out for Jesus and is inspiring others to follow his example. He's heading to the many frontlines in the world, yet he maintains a commitment to break down barriers within the church. He's taking preaching and pastoral leadership classes, leads a connect group, and is always thinking about the other "Steves" who need to be reached.

The tattoos on his arms speak of an incredible journey in Christ that has only just begun. As he talked, it was clear that Steve was prepared and called for a time such as this.

"I'm on a mission. I want to be a target and I know that only my faith will get me through."

Steve D'Agrosa

———

Steve D'Agrosa was born in Queens, New York, and lives in Manhattan. He attends Hillsong Church New York, where he is a volunteer staff member leading the 21+ age group, midweek services, and baptisms. Steve works for a charity called the Legacy Center, helping homeless people and poor families change their circumstances. He loves fishing with his dad and ballroom dancing, which he used to teach. Steve's passion is people, and he wants to change the culture of addiction and empty dreams that nearly killed him. Steve is in the process of having his story turned into a screenplay and book so others can see they don't need to be bound by the fear of addiction and can return to living a normal life.

Connect with Steve at stevedagrosa.com

CONTEMPLATION

But then *something happened*: God our Savior and His overpowering love and kindness for humankind entered our world; He came to save us. It's not that *we earned it* by doing good works or righteous deeds; He came because He is merciful.

TITUS 3:4–5

I have been crucified with the Anointed One—I am no longer alive—but the Anointed is living in me; and whatever life I have left in this failing body I live by the faithfulness of God's Son, the One who loves me and gave His body *on the cross* for me.

GALATIANS 2:20

The beginning of the biblical story sets the stage for all that follows. We meet the actors in this drama: the all-knowing, all-powerful Creator, the creatures, both animal and human, and the arch villain. We also learn about the critical elements of the drama. God reveals His true nature. He loves us and sets about calling us to Himself. Throughout the Bible and in the lives of believers down through the centuries, we see the character of God and His relentless pursuit of people, their struggle for survival, and the presence of evil. All our individual stories form a great narrative of God's unending love.

Use the following questions and Scripture passages to explore the truths revealed in the various articles, passages, and photographs found in this chapter. You may think through these questions alone, but we encourage you to discuss them with a friend or in a group. Truth becomes clearer as we seek it with others, and it is through the eyes of those who know us that we can see ourselves with greater clarity. The biblical account always becomes personal if we allow God to speak to us.

1. When you think about the creation narrative, what are the various things you learn about God's character and the nature of humans?

2. Why do you think choice is so essential to God's love and essential in our response to His love? What would you call love without choice?

3. John Milton said, "Gratitude bestows reverence." What does that mean and why is reverence so important in our response to God?

4. In Ephesians 2:14, Paul says that Jesus is the embodiment of our peace. Why do you think personal peace and peace within the Christian community is important? How does peace result from God's expression of love toward us? Is it possible to have true peace apart from God's mercy?

5. What do you think was driving Steve D'Agrosa to a life of addiction? Why was it so hard for Steve to hear the Christian message?

6. Why was it important for Steve to feel he had hit rock bottom in his life? What was it about the girl from the church connection team that finally cut through Steve's barriers?

7. What in Steve's conversation with Pastor Carl allowed him to feel he was finally welcome?

8. When have you faced or felt something that has kept you from feeling welcome? What made you feel like an outsider?

9. Is there something now or in your past that makes it difficult for you to accept that God truly loves you? What makes it so difficult for you to accept God's love?

10. Read Ephesians 1:4–5 again. What is God's desire for your life? What is so comforting about knowing God has adopted us to be His children?

Other Bible references for you to consider:

Jeremiah 31:3
Isaiah 54:6–7
1 Peter 1:3–7
Lamentations 3:22–24

THE FAITH ADVENTURE

———

Abram believed God *and trusted in His promises,* so God counted it to his favor as righteousness.

GENESIS 15:6

Words: Rebecca Newton VanDijk / Photography: Blaine Nadeau

The account of Abraham is a powerful example of God's faithfulness. Abraham is everything we aspire to be—courageous, brave, full of faith, and living a life of adventure. He's also everything we are—confused, uncertain, wavering, and at times, a very bad decision maker! Through the example given to us in God's relationship with Abraham, there is much revealed about the nature of God and His plans for our own personal relationship with Him.

God's Promises and Faithfulness Are Based on What He Has Done—Not What We Do

God did not bless Abraham (formerly Abram) and make a covenant with him because he obeyed God. God told Abraham to leave his country and declared:

> I have plans to make a great people from your descendants. And I am going to put a *special* blessing on you and cause your reputation to grow so that you will become a blessing *and example to others.* I will also bless those who bless you *and further you in your journey,* and I'll

trip up those who try to trip you *along the way. Through your descendants*, all of the families of the earth will find their blessing in you. (Gen. 12:2–3)

Then Abraham obeyed God. God didn't make this commitment as a result of Abraham's actions. God's promises were not about Abraham's actions but about His own faithfulness.

Even better, this promise made to Abraham was not exclusive. It was unique in being the first of its kind, but this promise is one God now makes to us all who believe.

> This is why, *you see*, *God saw* [Abraham's] faith *and* counted him as righteous; *this is how he became* right with God. The story of how faith was credited to Abraham was not recorded for him and him alone, but was written for all of us who would one day be credited for having faith in God. (Rom. 4:22–24)

We hear God's promises over our own lives, written for us in the Bible, and we want to believe, but do we? Just like Abraham, who is championed

> "Even better, this promise made to Abraham was not exclusive. It was unique in being the first of its kind, but this promise is one God now makes to us all who believe."

as the "father of our faith," we all experience times when our faith grows and waivers and grows again. He immediately responded to God's command with unwavering faith.

Then he took matters into his own hands, just like we do sometimes.

Next thing we know, Abraham was instructing his wife to pretend she was his sister to protect himself and be treated well since he *expected* Pharaoh to take his wife, Sarah, as his own. That's an interesting decision for a man who just left everything and followed God, especially in response to God's promise that He would bless him and protect him. And he didn't just do it once—he did the same thing again later!

After God had promised him children, Abraham had a child with his wife's servant, as this seemed the most likely way of making God's promises happen. Just like Abraham, we can be full of faith one minute, then trying to problem-solve and take matters into our own hands the next—when all along, God says He has a plan.

Despite Abraham's mistakes (and ours), God still kept His promises. And He keeps His promises with us regardless of whether we act in accordance with our beliefs or not. All we need is to have faith that the actions of Jesus on our behalf made us right with God.

Faith Means Knowing You Can Call on the Name of God, Whether You've Acted According to Your Faith or Not

We can always come back to God. And His promises stand. Abraham *knew* this. He knew his God. So instead of being full of regret and remorse and self-punishment after doing

something so extremely against God's plan for him, Abram, after being sent packing by Pharaoh, was once again blessed by God and "*He returned* to one of the first altar tables he had made *in the land,* stopped there, and called on the name of the Eternal *once again*" (Gen. 13:4).

Sometimes when we make bad choices, we think we're not worthy of calling on God. But we are. When we mess up, our relationship with God—made available simply through faith in the work of Jesus on our behalf—still stands. Abraham is an incredible example of faith not only because he chose to believe God's promises and acted immediately but also because when he messed up (and he really, really messed up), he knew he still had the *right* to call on the name of the Lord immediately.

Not only is it okay to call on God regardless of where we're at and how we're doing, but *it's also what God wants*. He gives us the example of Abraham so we know we can always turn to Him. He is there for us.

With Faith in God, We Can Relax

The pressure and stress of life can seem overwhelming. We've all felt it. The number of people on medication to deal with depression, anxiety, and stress is staggering. Sometimes we feel like shutting down and giving up, or we self-protect and become incredibly calculating and controlling of our lives and others around us.

That's when we should relax and give our stress to God.

When Abram and his nephew Lot needed to separate and go different ways because they were growing so great in number, Abram was so relaxed! We would understand if he felt stressed at this decision, as it seemingly had the potential to determine his future. But Abram was calm and easy about the decision-making process because he knew who determines his future.

A vast land is out there and available to you. It is time for us to go our separate ways. *You choose your land.* If you choose east, I'll go west. If you choose west, I'll go east—*it's your call.* (Gen. 13:9)

He could be this relaxed because he knew God would be true to His promises, regardless of the decision that was made between relatives. And God was.

Time and time again we see Abram relaxed in his certainty of God's faithfulness. When offered a great reward by the king of Sodom for his role in defeating his enemies, he refused, wanting his life to be a testimony to the promises and power of God alone. Regardless of what is going on around us, or the decisions we face before us, we can relax in God's faithfulness.

It's Okay to Get Personal

When Abram was still waiting for a child, God said to him, "Do not be afraid, Abram. I am *always* your shield *and protector*. Your reward *for loyalty and trust* will be immense" (Gen. 15:1).

Abram's words were less than gracious, but it was an honest response: "Eternal Lord, what could You *possibly* give to me *that would make that much of a difference in my life*? After all, I am still childless, and Eliezer of Damascus stands to inherit all I own. Since You have not given me the gift of children, my only heir will be one *of the servants* born in my household" (15:2–3).

As the years go on, Abram became more and more concerned that he didn't have any children. He was not responding to God's topic of conversation here; he was interrupting it! He was sharing with God his pain and despair, his heartache. He was talking to God personally about the fact that he was not a dad yet and wanted to be. God immediately responded and said that he would be, and Abram believed Him, which God, in turn, recognized: "Abram believed God *and trusted in His promises,* so God counted it to his favor as righteousness" (15:6).

Abraham was a friend of God, and by faith we have access to that same relationship. We know God in many different ways— as our creator, our savior, our hope, our provider, our healer. He is also our friend and confidante—intimate, personal, and caring.

Jesus Was Always God's Plan

In one of the most illuminating accounts in the Bible, Abraham, at the request of God, took his own son (whom he had longed for, treasured, and through whom he anticipated seeing the promises of God for his own life fulfilled) to offer him as a sacrifice. It seems impossible that he would do this. But he was certain of his God, of His ways being higher—even when we can't understand—and of His faithfulness to fulfill His promises, even when we can't see a way. In responding to his son's questions, "God will provide the lamb for the burnt offering, my son" (Gen. 22:8), Abraham declared a truth that will go on to echo through eternity: "*God Himself will provide the sacrifice.*"

This father-son relationship shows the sacrifice that God Himself was prepared to make—for *us*. Abraham's belief in God's faithfulness made him right with God. Our belief in God's faithfulness does too. In Jesus Christ, God Himself provided the sacrifice for our wrongdoings so that we might live in right relationship with Him, not based on what we do, but on what *He has done*—so that we might call on the name of the Lord. So that we can relax in our walk with God, day in, day out, seeking Him first and knowing the rest will follow. So that we, incredibly, can be personal and intimate with God Himself. Because Jesus was always God's plan— His plan for us to live in relationship with Him.

Faith isn't a concept, an idea, or a thing. Abraham shows us that faith comes out of relationship. It comes as a gift. And it certainly promises a life of adventure.

Rebecca Newton VanDijk

———

Rebecca is a social and organizational psychologist, committed to helping people develop themselves and empower others. She serves as an advisor, teacher, and coach to leaders globally, and lives in London with her husband and two children.

"We know God in many different ways— as our creator, our savior, our hope, our provider, our healer. He is also our friend and confidante—intimate, personal, and caring."

THE GIRL IN THE SPOTLIGHT

—

LOCATION: SYDNEY, AUSTRALIA

Words: Megan Butel / Photography: River Bennett
Stylist: Renae Bartley / Make-up: Anneke Knock

It took a few attempts for me to organize an interview with Tracy. She was busy with rehearsals for the annual church Christmas concert, where she was due to perform a solo.

I saw her at the concert before I spoke to her in person. Sitting there in the darkness was a welcome relief from the holiday chaos that surrounded the Christmas period. Little children spun their glow sticks incessantly as Tracy stepped out into the spotlight. She was dressed in a full-length gown with jewels sparkling around her neck. She enjoined us, in the words of the well-known carol, to "hail the heaven-born Prince of Peace."

She was both beautiful and talented. You could be forgiven for enviously wanting to be Tracy as she glittered in the spotlight. There were hundreds of families watching her stunning performance. Tracy's parents were not among them. Twelve years ago, four days after her eighth birthday, Tracy's father shot her mother dead and then committed suicide.

I met up with Tracy two days later at the local shopping mall and she shared her story with me. "My parents were very abusive toward each other," she told me, "particularly my dad toward my mom. At the age of four, I was also sexually abused by a friend of my dad's who we were living with at the time. As a result, my brother and I were placed together in an orphanage, but we were still allowed to visit our parents on weekends."

Tracy described what must have been a very confusing existence for a little girl. She lived at the orphanage but had contact with foster families and weekend visits with her parents. Her mother worked very hard to earn money to provide for the children, but alcohol abuse cast a dark shadow over the family.

"I remember walking across the railway tracks with my mother. It was quite a dodgy part of town, and we would go into these shacks that reeked of beer so she could buy some. We then walked all the way back home while she drank from the bottle. By three o'clock in the afternoon, she'd be out—completely unconscious. But I don't blame her for that. My grandfather was an alcoholic and died on a park bench from alcohol poisoning; my grandmother also drank a lot. My mother's childhood was very disruptive."

Tracy continued sadly, "The only time my parents were abusive toward each other was when they were both drunk. My father threatened my mother numerous times, but she was quite dependent on alcohol and I think that she was more afraid of being alone. My father being like that made less sense to me because it seemed like his childhood was pretty regular."

Tracy's father is a complex part of the story. She is uncertain how her father, originally from Britain, ended up in South Africa married to her mother and living in a "colored" neighborhood. She agrees that a white man living in that part of town would have been highly visible and a potential target for violence in the post-apartheid years. Her father seemed to like the thrill of risk-taking.

Tracy vividly remembers her father showing her a large scar where he had been stabbed while working as a police officer. "I very much saw my dad as a hero. He had been a police officer and a firefighter and a medical emergency responder. He always put himself in a position where he could be a hero. He's still a hero in my eyes despite what happened, because he was mentally ill at the time he did it."

Tracy recently discovered her father took other types of risks. She found out just this year that she has two half sisters as the result of an extramarital affair soon after she was born. "It's weird because they're twins and they look

"My grandfather was an alcoholic and died on a park bench from alcohol poisoning; my grandmother also drank a lot. My mother's childhood was very disruptive."

just like me," she said. "My mom actually knew about them, but she still stuck around—I think because of my brother and me. People ask me, 'Do you hate your parents for what happened and for how you were raised?' but I don't, because if you live with that hate, you don't live at all."

At some point, though, Tracy's mother did take steps to separate from her husband and she asked for a divorce. She also obtained a court interdict against him. The children were told on their last Sunday visit about the divorce. The next day, Tracy's father entered the store where her mother worked. Horrified staff and customers saw him come up behind her, place a gun to her head, and shoot. He then turned the gun on himself and collapsed on the floor next to her.

Fortunately for Tracy and her brother, they were safe at the orphanage. Both took the news differently. Tracy went into a state of silence, her brother into a state of anger.

"I remember the exact moment they broke the news. We were sitting on my bed in the girls' dormitory. They came in and locked the door. I just knew because there were police everywhere and my mom's best friend was standing there, staring at me. They told us what happened, and my brother's first reaction was to rip up my dad's photo." She smiled inadvertently and continued. "It was kind of funny because it was laminated so he couldn't tear it." All her poor brother could do was twist the image of his father back and forth in his small hands.

Tracy and her brother were sent to live for six months with one of their foster families. At the mention of her foster mother, Colleen, Tracy's face bursts into a radiant smile. It was Colleen who first told her about Jesus and how having him in her life could make all the difference. Tracy had to process the notion of a loving God against her experiences. She spent a long time being angry at Him for what had happened to her, and she was haunted by frequent nightmares involving her dead parents.

The six months spent with Colleen were an idyllic respite, as they lived in a lovely apartment by the beach and attended a private school. Her time there enabled Tracy to make her peace with God. Eventually, Tracy's maternal aunt took custody of the children and they were back living in an unsafe neighborhood and attending the local public school.

"At night, there was the sound of gunshots and houses being broken into—but it was still a home, though" she said softly.

After three years, another aunt came to visit. She told Tracy and her brother that she wanted to take them to Australia. She and her husband became their legal guardians and paid a large sum to enable them to emigrate from South Africa and join their family in Australia. Tracy found herself in strange new surroundings and at a private Christian school, where a new friend invited her to come to the youth group at her local church.

"I remember the first time standing there and I was absolutely overwhelmed. It was a special worship event and I heard the music and I was standing at the back, thinking, *What is this?* I started to cry. You could feel it. That was the night I gave my life to Jesus."

Tracy embarked on a journey of faith and enjoyed becoming a part of the church family. In her senior year of high school, she made a decision to get more serious about her involvement at church but got sideswiped by a serious bout of depression.

"It was kind of embarrassing," she said, "because the one thing I never wanted to be was a victim, but I had sort of fallen into a victim mentality with everything that had happened to me." This, combined with the usual pressures of the final year of high school, forced Tracy to pull back and put up emotional walls, but there was also a spiritual dimension involved. "It happened when I started singing in church," she explained. "I decided to get heavily involved in worship, and the more I got involved, the worse I started to feel. I felt very alone. I was put on antidepressants, but that made me feel worse about myself. Physically, I was feeling really sick all the time. I wasn't sleeping and I'd get hot and cold sweats. I was afraid to bring it up with the leaders. I didn't want to let people in or to be vulnerable."

The youth leaders noticed all was not well and raised the issue with Tracy. With their encouragement and support, she decided to step back from leadership while she sought help. "It

"People ask me, 'Do you hate your parents for what happened and for how you were raised?' but I don't, because if you live with that hate you don't live at all."

> "I was a testimony of strength and a testimony of His love. I've learned that your past doesn't have to define your future."

was embarrassing to have people ask me why I wasn't singing anymore," she admitted. "After a nine or ten-month break, I got involved with stage managing. It was so exciting to be involved again. The leadership lifted my responsibilities off me, but the people never left me. It was awesome to be back on the team. Slowly, I got involved with the choir again, and the first time I sang with them, I cried. I'd never realized before that it was what God wanted me to do. Lots of people have told me, 'You're called to lead. You're called to worship.'

"I realized that everyone around me had my back. At a time when I was really struggling, they were family. Family is more than blood. They stood by me through thick and thin, and they helped me and they pushed me, in a good way, to get better. One of the conditions of me staying on as a leader was to talk to someone and get help. Four years on, I'm still in contact with my counselor. We catch up for coffee, and she's become like a mother to me. My church family also embraces my real family. My brother recently got into a bit of trouble, and they were all praying for him. My aunt and uncle aren't believers, but when they come to church with me, everyone makes a special effort to be really warm and welcoming."

Through all the trials, Tracy has come to a sense of peace. "I realized that through everything that happened it was never God's intention that I would get hurt. Apart from the abuse I suffered when I was little, I've never been physically harmed and I've come through stronger. I came to this realization that God placed every single person in my life for a reason.

"One day, my housemates and I had to move out of our house, and I had lost my job. I said to God, 'You brought me here—you get me out of this!' It wasn't a super spiritual 'I trust you, God'; it was a bit more like a dummy spit."

"Then I felt Him say, 'You're going to share your story,' and I said, 'No, I'm not.' The very next week, I was asked to share my story at a big youth event. I burst into tears when I was asked because I had doubted God but He never doubted me.

"The first time I shared my story on stage, nobody knew. At the end, I was surprised when everyone clapped. Afterward, a young girl came up to me in tears and said, 'You have no idea how much hope you've given me. I was sexually abused for a very long time and you've been through a lot more than me, but you've made it. You're a testimony of strength.' It really hit me—this is my story. God gave me my voice to put me in a position, a spotlight, so that I could share my story. I found peace in the weirdest moment because I wasn't a victim anymore. I was a testimony of strength and a testimony of His love. I've learned that your past doesn't have to define your future."

We said good-bye to each other in a sea of last-minute Christmas shoppers. Amidst the cacophony of sound, I heard Christmas carols playing over the loudspeakers. We may be obscured by the noise of everyday life, but Jesus, the Prince of Peace, is still present.

Tracy Pratt

———

Tracy was born in Cape Town, South Africa, and now lives in Sydney, Australia. She is currently at the Hillsong International College studying songwriting and is part of the church worship team. Tracy is passionate about life, exploring, and pushing herself beyond what she ever thought possible. She wants to be someone who encourages others to always believe in themselves and pursue their dreams against the odds.

CONTEMPLATION

After all, it is I, the Eternal One your God,
who has hold of your right hand,
Who whispers *in your ear,*
"Don't be afraid. I will help you."

ISAIAH 41:13

Your love, O Eternal One, towers high into the heavens.
Even the skies are lower than Your faithfulness.
Your justice is like the majestic mountains,
Your judgments are as deep as the oceans, *and yet in Your greatness,*
You, O Eternal, offer life for every person and animal.

PSALM 36:5–6

The relationship that Abraham had with God was very special. He was known as the friend of God, but it could also be said that God was the friend of Abraham. Paul later holds Abraham up as the model for our faith. Faith on the part of Abraham and faithfulness on the part of God was the foundation of this relationship.

Later, Abraham's faith relationship concerning Isaac provides insight into the depth of God's friendship as shown in the Father's gift of His Son's sacrifice made for sin. It is all about relationship, and the result is confidence we have in the love of God.

Use the following questions and Scripture passages to understand the fullness of God as our Father and friend. Spend time alone with these questions and then discuss them with your friends to grow deeper in your relationship with God.

---

1. How is the concept of the word *believe* that Abraham exhibited in his dealings with God different than what we normally understand the word *believe* to mean in our dealings with other people or believing a set of facts?

2. Why is Abraham considered the "father of our faith"? Do you have someone whom you consider to be your spiritual parent?

3. What does it mean when God keeps His promises unconditionally? Can you give an example in your life or the life of someone you know when God kept His promise, although He would have been justified if He had not kept it?

4. In this section, it says, "Sometimes we feel like shutting down and giving up, or we self-protect and become incredibly calculating and controlling of our lives and others around us" Can you think of ways in which you or others you know do this?

5. What does it mean to "relax in God's faithfulness"? How is this opposite of our normal tendency to react in a crisis?

6. How is faith a gift of God? Can you explain how faith is learned through relationships rather than developed solely by logic?

7. Tracy experienced a traumatic shock with the murder-suicide of her parents, resulting in her withdrawal, and ceased to communicate. What caused her to break out of this behavior and then to realize she was seeing herself as a victim? When have you or someone you know had to face personal victimization?

8. Tracy finally had to realize that family was more than blood. Can you identify who outside of your blood relations is truly family in your life? Is this closeness outside of family relationship true for others around you?

9. What difficult things have you faced that you can say God had a reason (for good) for bringing these difficulties into your life?

10. What things must you still face before you can truly say your past will not determine your future?

Other Bible references for you to consider:

Psalm 89:24–37
Hebrews 10:19–25
Revelation 2:9–10
John 6:35–40

CHAPTER THREE: THE ONE

THE HELPER

———

I will ask the Father to send you another Helper,
the Spirit of truth, who will remain constantly with you.
The world does not recognize the Spirit of truth,
because it does not know the Spirit and is unable to receive Him.
But you do know the Spirit because He lives with you, and
He will dwell in you. I will never abandon you like
orphans; I will return to be with you.

JOHN 14:16–18

Words: Carlos Darby / Photography: Chelsea Crosby

W e live in a world full of orphans. They mostly have a family, but spiritually speaking they're not yet part of the family of God. It's a strange idea to think that before we entered into a relationship with Jesus, we were just that—orphans, wandering through life, searching to be welcomed home into the family of God. We were in darkness and called into the glorious light, called to enter through an open door (Christ Jesus), where on the other side our spiritual family was waiting.

Paul says in Ephesians 1:5, "He destined us to be adopted as His children through *the covenant* Jesus the Anointed *inaugurated in His sacrificial life*. This was His pleasure and His will *for us*."

Adoption has always been at the heart of God's plan for humanity, that through Jesus we would once again be part of His family for eternity.

Jesus told His disciples near the end of the book of John, "I will never abandon you like orphans; I will return to be with you. In a little while, the world will not see Me; but I will not vanish completely from your sight. Because I live, you will also live" (John 14:18–19). I think He could tell that they were starting to feel anxious. They had followed Him for years, had seen amazing miracles, and had been given purpose and guidance. Now He was saying that He would no longer be there, that He was going to leave them.

I think we can all relate to sometimes feeling alone, when we need guidance, a reminder of why we're here, whom we're following, and why we're living. Jesus could have just said, "Listen, I'm going to heaven to be with the Father. I'll be watching and will be involved in your life—but from afar."

Thank God that Jesus died so that we could enter into the relationship through faith in Him and enter into His family. But we get something more, or should I say, *Someone*. We were orphans; we know what it's like to not be in a relationship with Jesus; therefore, we know that sense of abandonment that comes from being separated from the family. We can sometimes forget that we are no longer orphans and can act like ones, searching for identity and meaning outside of whom we really are in Christ Jesus and who we have with us constantly.

The Helper

> Because you, too, have heard the word of truth—the good news of your salvation—and because you believed *in the One who is truth*, your lives are marked with His seal. This is *none other than* the Holy Spirit who was promised as the guarantee toward the inheritance we are to receive when He frees and rescues all who belong to Him. To God be all praise and glory! (Eph. 1:13–14)

Jesus wasn't going to leave His disciples, and He won't just leave us now. We aren't going to have a pen pal in heaven who we can write to when we need something or when we want to share what's happening in our lives. We have been given the Holy Spirit who resides in us.

Unfortunately, the Holy Spirit could be the most ignored person in our lives, but He's the most important person in experiencing Jesus, because the major function of the Holy Spirit is to point to Jesus. He's also called our helper, our teacher; he reveals the mind of God toward us. Jesus says:

> At that time, you will know that I am in the Father, you are in Me, and I am in you. The one who loves Me will do the things I have commanded. My Father loves everyone who loves Me; and I will love you and reveal My heart, will, and nature to you. (John 14:20–21)

Loving Jesus every day is a fruit of reminding ourselves how much He loves us, what He's done, and how He actually lives with us every day. He's given us the Holy Spirit to help us stay focused on His love so we will love Him back and can therefore see His heart, will, and nature.

The Holy Spirit also convicts, comforts, and speaks to us to act. He's there to be involved in our lives. He's not there to sit at the sidelines. God gave us the Holy Spirit so we'd be reminded that we are no longer orphans; we have been adopted. He's a seal to prove that our identity is now a part of a royal household in the kingdom of heaven.

Acknowledging Him is part of being in a relationship with Jesus, because we're submitting to His voice, because He speaks through the Holy Spirit. If we ignore the Holy Spirit, we're ignoring Jesus. When we acknowledge Him, asking for wisdom, strength, and understanding, we're validating our relationship with Him.

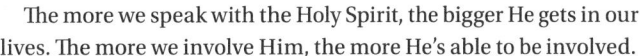

The more we speak with the Holy Spirit, the bigger He gets in our lives. The more we involve Him, the more He's able to be involved.

Hardness of Heart Leads to Inexperience

But this is not *the path of* the Anointed One, which you have learned. If you have heard Jesus and have been taught by Him according to the truth that is in Him, then you know to take off your former way of life, your *crumpled* old self—*that dark blot of a soul* corrupted by deceitful desire and lust— *to take a fresh breath* and to let God renew your attitude and spirit. Then *you are ready to* put on your new self, modeled after the very likeness of God: truthful, righteous, and holy. (Eph. 4:20-24)

This biggest challenge in my journey with Jesus and experiencing Him is making sure that I play my part in keeping my heart soft and that I don't forget who I am now: adopted, loved, and sealed with the Holy Spirit.

He is the connection to heaven, He knows the mind of Jesus, and therefore we can know His will. We all want guidance, to be led by the Spirit, but a major factor that can prevent us from experiencing Him is a hardness of heart. When our hearts start going hard because we live from our old orphan nature, the voice of the Holy Spirit can become muted and our sense of the presence of God can become desensitized.

The old orphan nature can become more prevalent, and a sense of abandonment can creep in, where we start ignoring our relationship with Jesus and therefore our Father in heaven. John puts it like this:

Anyone who denies the Son does not know the Father. The one affirming the Son enjoys an intimate relationship with the Father as well.

Let *the good news*, the story you have heard from the beginning of your journey, live in *and take hold of* you. If that happens *and you focus on the good news*, then you will always remain in a relationship with the Son and the Father. This is what He promised us: eternal life.

I also am writing to warn you about some who are attempting to deceive you. You have an anointing. You received it from Him, and His anointing remains on you. You do not need any other teacher. But as His anointing instructs you in all *the essentials* (all the truth uncontaminated by darkness and lies), it teaches you this: "Remain connected to Him." (I John 2:23–27)

As we saw in the Garden of Eden, it is lies that harden our heart to the truth. Adam's and Eve's hearts were hardened and turned from the true nature of God, which was to protect and love them. Because we have a free will, our part in keeping a healthy relationship with Jesus through the Holy Spirit is by keeping a soft heart and hardening our heart to the lies that come at us. The times when we can let offense take root, when feeling important can become an addiction, pretty much everything that hardens a heart toward Jesus is a result of exalting something in our lives to higher in our thinking than Jesus. The answer is that the good news will take hold of our hearts. It's like an ointment for the heart; it keeps it supple, where the presence of Jesus is felt, and it brings joy and a short memory when it comes to offense, guilt, and condemnation.

Let's be encouraged that we can't produce the fruit of the Spirit by trying to be patient and kind in our own strength. It's fruit that only comes through the good news taking hold of our hearts. It's the fruit that draws us closer to Jesus and shows Jesus to our world. Keeping Jesus and His message central by guarding our hearts against lies keeps it soft and attentive to the voice of the Holy Spirit, and it is always encouraging us to experience Jesus.

When the right time arrived, God sent His Son into this world (born of a woman, subject to the law) to free those who, *just like Him*, were subject to the law. Ultimately, He wanted us all to be adopted as sons and daughters. Because you are now part of God's family, He sent the Spirit of His Son into our hearts; *and the Spirit* calls out, "Abba, Father." (Gal. 4:4–6)

"The answer is that the good news
will take hold of our hearts. It's like an
ointment for the heart; it keeps it supple."

A LIFE AND DEATH DECISION

———

LOCATION: LONDON, UK

Words: Cate Burton / Photography: Andreas Smitz

Sandra lives in London with her eighteen-year-old daughter, Natalia, and this story is as much about her as it is about Sandra. If Sandra had listened to the voice of society and the people she loved the most, Natalia would not be here.

Born into a large middle-class family in Brazil, Sandra was involved in church from a young age.

"The whole family on my mother's side was Catholic. My mom was converted when I was about eight years old, and from then on we regularly attended an Evangelical church."

Sandra met Natalia's father at church when she was fifteen. "We didn't have a physical relationship, but we were dating," she recalled. "When I look back now, I think I kind of substituted my father, as he was slightly older. There were no problems with our relationship, but one day in church I had this strong feeling that I needed to break up with him. He did nothing wrong, nothing had happened; I just had this strong conviction that I could not ignore."

Sandra's father left when she was about sixteen years old, and the family moved from a comfortable position in life to a place of struggle.

"I was lucky enough to finish school that year," Sandra continued. "I was due to take entry exams for university, but we couldn't afford them. I'd always wanted to study archaeology, but there was no way we could afford it. My school was fantastic. They praised my writing ability and encouraged me to study journalism. I could only afford one entry, and it was to a university in the South. It was a government-run university, and you didn't have to pay for it; however, you had forty people competing for each individual place on the course.

"I prayed to God to help me. I had no idea what was going to happen, but I applied for the course. Just before I went to take the entry exam, I got back together with my ex." The relationship had developed by this time and started to become more physical. "I didn't know what to do," Sandra said. "It did not feel right, but I had nobody I could talk to. Now I recognize that I definitely felt pressured. I was so young, and at the time

I thought I was being complimented. He made me feel like I was quite special to be receiving this kind of attention. In hindsight, I see that he was very possessive, but I just thought he was caring. I was sixteen and I honestly believed I was going to be with him for the rest of my life.

"The reality was not a fairy tale at all, and I got very depressed. I knew I'd made an awful mistake and I tried to get away from him. I didn't want to talk to him. I felt violated even though I had consented. It was just awful. I couldn't stop crying.

"I couldn't tell anyone. The church then was very different to the church I'm in now; it was very judgmental. I felt repulsive, humiliated, guilty, and ashamed.

"My only hope was university," Sandra recalled. "I felt if I left the city, then I wouldn't have to face up to it."

Sandra managed to pass her exams and was offered a place at university to study journalism, but there was another twist in the tale just around the corner.

"It was during this time that I discovered I was pregnant. I honestly never thought I would get pregnant, which was very naïve. Suddenly, we were planning a wedding. The story came out, and my family just wanted to fix things. People thought that if we were married it would make the whole situation slightly more acceptable.

"I was a scandal. I had people in the church telling me to my face I was a prostitute, but my biggest shock was the reaction of those closest to me. I had gone from golden girl to being branded a prostitute. I was just cast out."

Some of her friends suggested that she take matters into her own hands. "They told me, 'Oh, you have to have an abortion; you cannot have this baby,'" Sandra said. "'You know how difficult it is. You are one of the top students. Your life as you know it is finished right here if you have this baby.

"For me, an abortion was never an option. My friends said I was out of my mind. I remember them saying, 'You're never going to make it, and you'll never finish university.' It was all completely negative."

Sandra moved to a city in the south of Brazil to study, and her husband went with her. Her family refused to speak to her, so the two of them were alone and his true colors started to show.

"My education was the one thing that kept me going; it gave me something to hold on to. I had a job lined up, but I couldn't accept it because I was pregnant. I had no idea how I was going to manage financially. I had nothing. I didn't know at the time, but Natalia's father had a drug abuse problem. He never physically attacked me, but he became more and more obsessive. He was really angry that I had decided to move with or without him. Although he decided to come with me, he resented it very much."

Even though Sandra had moved, it became increasingly obvious that she would continue to experience the same prejudice and hatred that she had hoped to leave behind in her hometown.

"Our church did not accept me, because as far as they were concerned, I was guilty of my husband's downfall. It was really upsetting. We had nowhere to live and eventually ended up in a very secluded borough out the back of the church. There was pure poverty everywhere.

"We lived in one small room with bare brick walls. When it rained, the water came inside, and when it was hot, it was like an oven. There I was, four months pregnant in this secluded area with no proper roads. There was no water, just a well. I'd only ever seen these things on television. I could never have believed I would live like that. I cried day and night.

"I started university and I just prayed and kept going. Food was scarce, and having been cut off by my family, I had lost my private health insurance. I knew that God was looking after me. I was praying to Him, saying, 'I am not giving my baby enough. You have to look after her.'

"I would go to the library early in the morning and read books on nutrition and how to look after yourself. I read as much as I could; I would not be defeated. I was really tired, I had no money, and I was always hungry. I'd tell myself and my baby: 'You are not going to die. This is not it. Cry, scream, and do whatever you have to do, but I am not going to be one of the statistics. I refuse.' Things started to get really bad, though. My husband was not finding work, and when he did get a job, he would be fired

after one week. I still didn't know about his drug use so I couldn't understand what was happening.

"At this time, I met a lady from the church who lived in the same borough. She was very loving and she ended up looking after me for two months, inviting me for lunch and asking how I was. She was the first person I met who was completely nonjudgmental. I finally had somebody to talk to.

"Also, my cousin who lived in another city spoke with me. She told me that she felt God had spoken to her and that He wanted her to move to where I was. She was totally obedient and actually moved. She left her job and she moved to the city where I was. Suddenly, I had these two women offering me love and support."

It was fortunate that they were, because around this time, Sandra's husband became increasingly obsessive. "He would come to the university during my breaks and see who I was talking to," she shared. "One day, I decided that I had to leave him completely.

"I left university for the day, and he was there outside. He said to me, 'You have to come now; you have to come now.' I had this feeling that I should not go with him, but he took my bag from me and told me, 'You are coming with me!' I was eight months pregnant at this point, I had no money, and the campus was miles away, so I couldn't walk. I had no choice but to go with him.

"I felt like I was in danger and I had to calm myself down. There was a shelf just inside the entrance of our house and, as I approached it, the first thing I saw was a gun. I knew in that second that if I didn't cooperate, he could kill me. I started to pray and decided that I would wait until he fell asleep and then I would grab my things and leave.

"I just kept praying. I knew I couldn't fall asleep, but while I was still awake I had a very vivid image, a kind of dream. I had a friend who had died in a car accident just a few months before. In my vision, I was dressed in white and I was at the beach. My friend was right in the middle of the sea and I was looking at him and saying, 'I am coming to meet you. Today. I am coming.' It was really intense. We were talking back and forth, and he said, 'No, you're not coming today.'"

"I was a scandal. I had people in the church telling me to my face I was a prostitute, but my biggest shock was the reaction of those closest to me. I had gone from golden girl to being branded a prostitute. I was just cast out."

"Some of her friends suggested that she take matters into her own hands. "They told me, 'Oh, you have to have an abortion; you cannot have this baby,'" Sandra said "'You know how difficult it is, you are one of the top students. Your life as you know it is finished right here if you have this baby.'"

At this point in the interview, Sandra became visibly upset. She continued, "I told him, 'No, I want to come. I want to be where you are,' but he replied, 'It's not your time yet. Go back. Wake up!'

"At that moment, I woke up and my husband had fallen asleep. Within seconds, I had taken my bag and rushed to the door. It was 5:00 a.m., and the first bus was just coming. He came after me; it was like a horror movie. He was running after me, and it was the scariest thing I've ever experienced, but I escaped!"

Sandra managed to get on a bus and made it to her cousin's house. When she got there, she told her what had happened. "My cousin spoke with my husband," Sandra recalled. "She told him that if he tried to come around me, he would get arrested. I didn't speak to him again for a long time, but I was obviously quite traumatized by the whole thing."

Shortly after moving into her cousin's house, Sandra gave birth to her daughter. However, it was anything but a predictable birth.

"When I went into labor and gave birth, I didn't feel anything!" Sandra recalled. "I had no contractions—nothing. On the day I had my last antenatal appointment with my doctor, he was examining me and said, 'Sandra, are you not feeling anything?' I told him no and that I felt fine, just a little tired. He just looked at me and said,

'Your water broke! When did your water break?' I actually argued with him! I told him, 'No, it didn't. It didn't break.' Surely I would have noticed."

The doctor knew better and called a nurse to lie Sandra down. "It was all very shocking, but very quick," she said. "Everyone was shouting, 'Oh my God! What are we going to do? Is the baby okay? It's a big baby; she can't be delivered natural; this girl is too small.' I wasn't having contractions, so I couldn't push. I wasn't in any pain. I had been completely oblivious to the fact I was in labor!"

Natalia was eventually born by caesarean section. Sandra's prayers obviously paid off as Natalia weighed in at a very healthy ten pounds with no signs of malnourishment or problems relating to the pregnancy.

Around the same time as Natalia's birth, Sandra's mother had a change of heart and showed up. It was the start of a long and slow restoration in that relationship. "We said nothing," Sandra recalled. "We had no words. Now we have a very good relationship. I talk to her three times a week, but then, nothing. We didn't even touch. There was nothing that could be said at that time. Since then she has been such a help. She came and stayed with me and moved around with me when it was necessary for work or study. God really turned my life around after that. I got incredibly exciting jobs as a journalist while I was still studying, and then in 2001, I came to the United Kingdom.

"My mother has always been a very traditional Christian, but her views have changed considerably. My life has been an example for her of grace and persistence."

Five years after Natalia's birth, Sandra finally managed to track down her husband to finalize their divorce. He had seen Natalia briefly just after she was born, but she didn't meet him properly until she was fifteen.

"He was always very difficult to find," Sandra said. "When I did find him and meet with him, I actually felt compassion for him. When we were together, he was a very good-looking man, but now his face was hard, almost disfigured. After I left, he hadn't needed to control himself anymore. His abuse became so serious that his family had to get an intervention. At the time we met, he had been clean for four years and had trained as a hairdresser. He also had a new wife. I told him, 'God is giving you another chance. Do it right.'

"He never acknowledged what he had put me through. He never said sorry. It's like it never happened. He did tell me that when he was at his lowest he would always remember how I kept going with things even when everyone was against me. He said that gave him motivation to study and move forward with his life. That really touched me."

It's difficult to match this story with the beautiful, confident woman you see when you look at Sandra. "I'm not there yet," she said. "It's not finished, but I'm persistent in what's good. I am pleased with where I am now. I'm not rich, but I have everything I need. I'm here by the grace of God and nothing else. I know in my heart that I had to go through all those things to get to where I am today. Natalia is beautiful, and she is doing so well. Even though our life is not perfect, I know that we can get through anything."

If Sandra had listened to those around her, it could have been a very different story, but the lives they are living now are testimony to the fact that sometimes other people's opinions are not worth listening to. Sandra knew her heart and trusted it. She was strong in her convictions and pursued goodness.

Sandra Porto

Sandra Porto was born in Cuiaba, Mato Grosso, Brazil, and has lived in London since 2001. She attends Holy Trinity Brompton Church, where she's a volunteer leading Alpha groups. In her work life, Sandra is a freelance journalist and works in public relations. Sandra is passionate about justice and learning to appreciate the beauty around us. She never wants to stop learning and telling extraordinary stories about ordinary people.

CONTEMPLATION

You see, you have not received a spirit that returns you to slavery, so you have nothing to fear. The Spirit you have received adopts you *and welcomes you* into God's own family. That's why we call out to Him, "Abba! Father!" *as we would address a loving daddy. Through that prayer,* God's Spirit confirms in our spirits that we are His children. If we are God's children, that means we are His heirs along with the Anointed, set to inherit everything that is His. If we share His sufferings, *we know that* we will ultimately share in His glory.

ROMANS 8:15–17

I will give them *a new will*—an undivided heart—and plant a new spirit within them; I will remove their *cold*, stony heart and replace it with a *warm* heart of flesh. Then they will follow My commands and uphold My laws and *actually* do as I say. They will be My people, and I will be their God.

EZEKIEL 11:19–20

The great mystery of faith is that God has chosen us to be in His family. We are adopted brothers and sisters who share in God's inheritance. When life is at its darkest, we are still loved by our Father. We are children of God alongside Jesus, and now that Jesus is with the Father we have the Holy Spirit resident within us. Our role becomes to enjoy this unique position and to allow the Holy Spirit to fill us and guide us.

Use the following questions to consider the wonder of being adopted into God's family. Share with your friends any observations or questions you might have.

1. Why do you think Jesus described the Holy Spirit as another helper? Who was the first helper?

2. Why do you think we are called "adopted children" rather than just "children of God"? What is unique and comforting about being adopted?

3. What are some of the benefits of having the Holy Spirit reside within us? In your own life, have you experienced the presence of the Holy Spirit? Would you call Him a comfort to you? If not, how would you describe Him?

4. Paul encourages us to "take off your former way of life" and to "renew your attitude and spirit" (Eph. 4:22, 23) What things can you point to in your life that should be put off, and how should your attitude be changed?

5. Give examples that you have seen of soft and hard hearts.

How do these affect one's openness to God, and how do you go about changing the hardness of your heart?

6. In Sandra's story, she faced great difficulties and experienced rejection by some in her church. Have you ever experienced similar rejection or seen it in someone else's life? Why do you think some in the church felt the need to judge others?

7. In Sandra's life, one lady in her church and her cousin went out of their way to be supportive. When have you or someone you know had an opportunity to be an encouragement to someone in trouble? Have you been the recipient of similar encouragement?

8. Sandra was encouraged to abort her unwanted pregnancy. What are the implications of aborting or carrying through with the birth of a child in such difficult circumstances?

9. In this chapter, we see the promise of the Holy Spirit in the midst of Paul's encouragement to put off the old ways. At the same time, we see Sandra faced with living through difficult times and her unfortunate choices. How do these two narratives work together?

10. What can we do to make sure we are open to the work of the Holy Spirit? How do we go about changing our attitudes?

Other Bible references for you to consider:

2 Corinthians 5:17–19
John 16:13–15
Psalm 30:4–5
Colossians 1:25–27

FAITH OF THE FATHERLESS

"Know this: children are a gift from the Eternal;
the fruit of the womb is His reward."

PSALM 127:3

Words: Alice Sullivan / Photography: Evan Rummel

F or years, any time I was at an event or even walking through downtown and spotted them, I'd stop and watch. They interacted—holding hands, laughing, enjoying the moment—unaware that they were on display as my curiosity ran wild. They were an anomaly as far as I was concerned. I was always a little skeptical of the sincerity, the permanence. And always a little sad, maybe a twinge of jealousy too, that I missed out on that part of life. Fathers spending time with their kids— the whole thing was a mystery to me. After a minute or two, I'd walk away, leaving them in peace. Leaving my heart in pieces.

Unfortunately, my story is all too familiar and prevalent. Abusive or absentee father, damaged child. Child grows up with a bevy of insecurities and daddy issues, grows to distrust others, becomes withdrawn, forms unhealthy relationships, projects all anger upon a mean and uncaring God. You wouldn't think that one relationship—or lack thereof—could have such far-reaching consequences, but it does.

When I was a little girl, I used my glow-in-the-dark cross bookmark as a nightlight. It was activated by heat so every night before bed I'd hold it over my bedside lamp until it was hot. Then I'd hang it on the wall, turn off the lights, jump into bed—covers up to my neck—and watch the glow fade until my eyes strained to see even the faintest outline of the cross. In my mind, I was only safe as long as I could see the cross. Bad things happened in the dark, and the light only lasted about thirty minutes. After that, God left the room. Left me alone.

As a seven-year-old, I rationalized that God didn't care about me. I went to Sunday school and repeated Bible stories while harboring this disconnect in my heart. When we learned how Jesus said, "Let the little children come to me," I was skeptical. Without a healthy role model at home of what a father is supposed to look like, these stories were just that—stories. On the other hand, I lived the reality at home.

When I'd spent two decades being mad and hurt, I had to admit I didn't want to spend another decade the same way. So I started searching for answers. And not from my earthly father—I'd long since given up on getting an apology or an explanation. In time, I even forgave him for his many indiscretions. But now, as an adult, I was ready for answers about myself. Who was I? What am I worth? I knew I couldn't magically undo the past, but I could begin to tear down each of my insecurities and rebuild my heart and my self-esteem based on the messages *I should have learned and heard* as a child. Yes, it would be hard work, but I knew I was worth it. Finally.

Just ask and it will be given to you; seek after it and you will find. *Continue to* knock and the door will be opened for you. (Matt. 7:7)

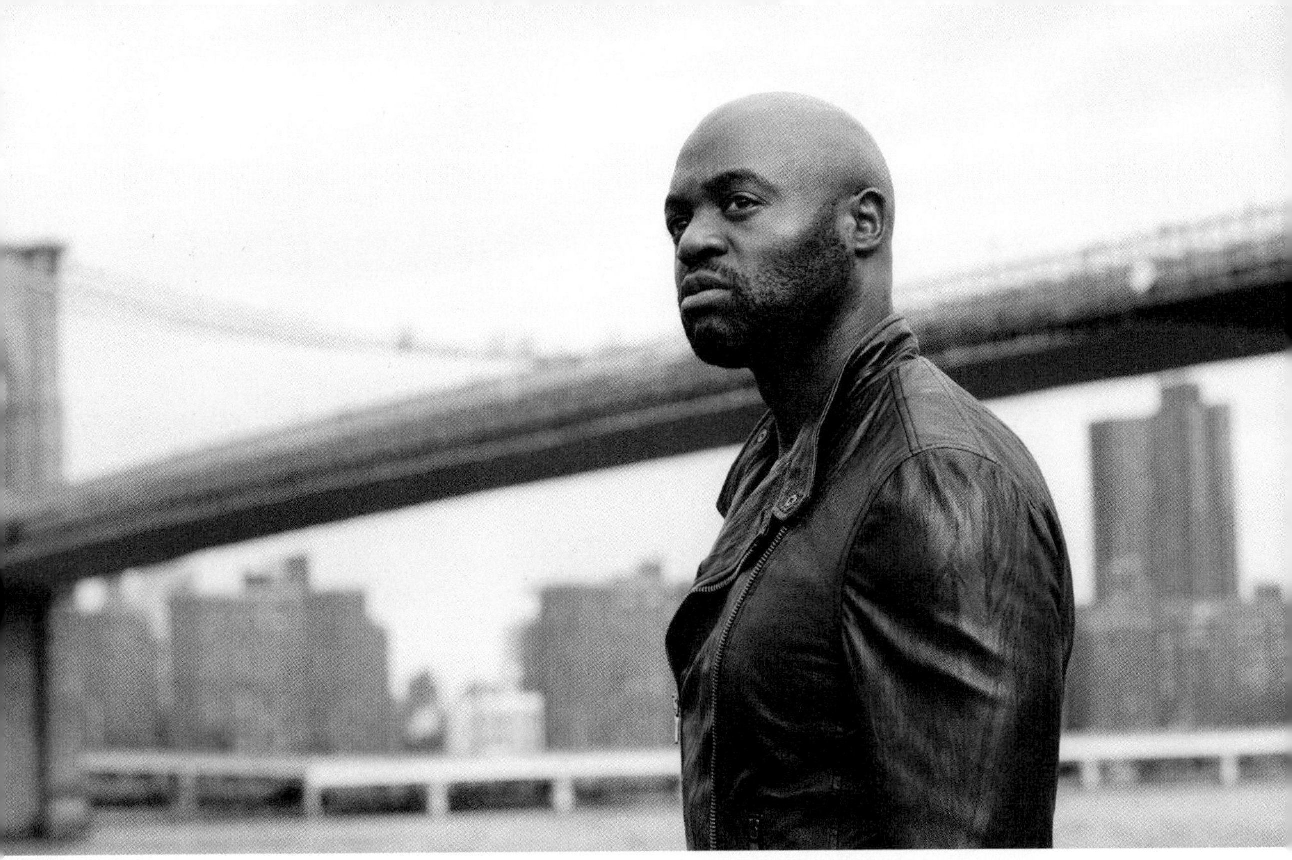

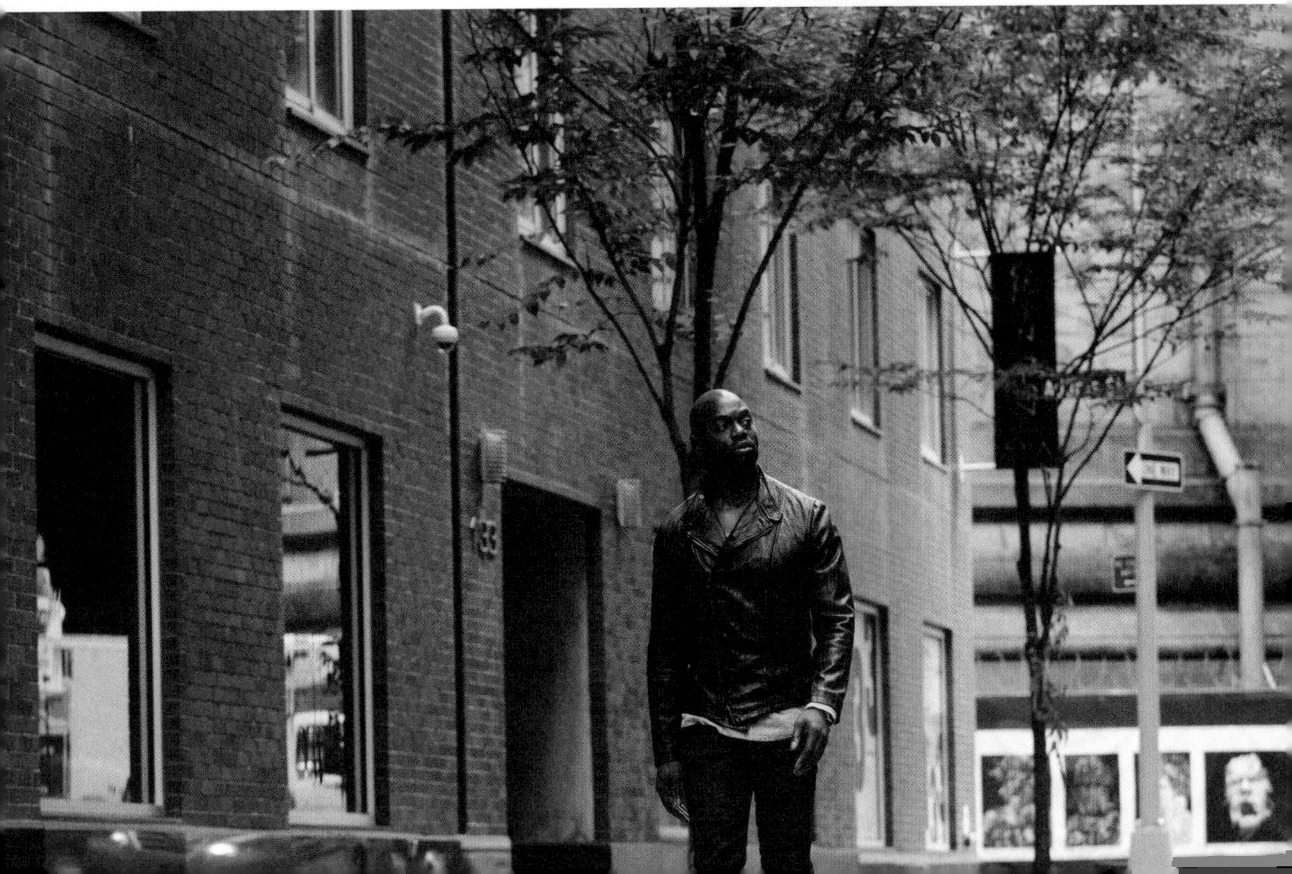
133

> "As the weeks and months passed, I learned to speak with Him in new, more comfortable ways, as though He's actually near me and listening, because He is. I'm also more expectant of an answer."

There was just one catch—I still had daddy issues—as in "Heavenly Father" issues. I may have forgiven my earthly father for all the things he did and didn't do, but I still had a deep grudge against God for allowing anything bad to happen in the first place.

One night when the pain was too great, I had a full-on argument with Him. I cried. I yelled. I blamed Him for not caring, not listening, not protecting me, not giving me an ideal childhood and life, for that matter. I pointed my finger and yelled some more. He was quiet, like I'd imagine a patient parent to be, watching their kid throw a tantrum. When I was done—I couldn't think of any more reasons to shout at Him—there was a silence and a peace. In the stillness, I felt that God wasn't mad at me. I only felt compassion and a nearly imperceptible whisper inside saying, "Now let's move forward together." He wasn't going anywhere. In fact, He was going to hang around whether I liked it or not. So I agreed to a truce.

If I was going to heal and become the healthy person I envisioned, I needed to know what the right messages were—what God actually says about me. I knew a lot of people who had great relationships with God, even if they didn't have a great relationship with one or both parents. So I began searching for scriptures. What I found made me reevaluate my grudge with God.

I am God's child. (Gal. 3:26)
I knew children should be protected, loved, and encouraged.

I am Jesus' friend. (John 15:15)
I valued my friendships and made time for them.

I am God's incredible work of art. (Eph. 2:10)
Art has great worth and every piece is unique and beautiful in its own way.

I am totally and completely forgiven. (1 John 1:9)
I could forgive myself and move on.

I am greatly loved. (Rom. 5:8)
If I was valuable and worthy of love, I wanted to be near the source.

Maybe God wasn't a bad guy after all. Maybe He deserved a second chance. And an apology.

As the weeks and months passed, I learned to speak with Him in new, more comfortable ways, as though He were actually near me and listening, because He was. I'm also more expectant of an answer.

I'm kinder to others and to myself. I've learned to forgive and move on. I know I'll have a much better example of how to love, encourage, and teach when I have a family of my own. And I've been able to see Him in everything, everywhere, especially in loving interactions within families. Even more so with fathers and their children.

Consider the kind of extravagant love the Father has lavished on us—He calls us children of God! It's true; we are His *beloved* children. And in the same way the world didn't recognize Him, the world does not recognize us either. (I John 3:1)

Though our stories may be different, the aftermath of faulty parenting is likely the same. The result is a generation of twenty- and thirty-somethings who has a distrust of authority figures, a fractured view of family, a low sense of value, and an unhealthy view of God. We think God is sitting on a cloud somewhere, completely unaware of what's happening down here, and when He does pop in for a few minutes, He plays favorites. But nothing could be more wrong.

He loves each one of us dearly. Each one. And He's right here! He's not on vacation or unavailable. Whether we're on the train, in our cars, or walking down the street, He's there, waiting and walking with us. He's a friend, a mentor, a Father. He wants to spend time with you, like a father would with his child. He's the ultimate example of a good parent.

While we may have been disappointed, abused, or abandoned by those we love, God—our Heavenly Father—will never leave us. And He's stronger than we give Him credit for being.

Be strong and brave, and don't tremble in fear of them, because the Eternal your God is going with you. He'll never fail you or abandon you! (Deut. 31:6)

The sight of dads playing with their kids still makes me pause. I hear a giggle and turn to see a dad chasing after his daughter, catching her amid happy shrieks. He swoops her up in his arms and kisses her head. And sometimes even while I'm smiling, I start to feel the tiniest tug of doubt, regret. My heart says, *Where were you, God? Why not me?*

Then just as fast, "I'm right here. And I love you."

Alice Sullivan

———

Alice Sullivan has worked in the book publishing industry since 2001 as a ghostwriter, author, writing coach, speaker, and editor and has worked on more than 1,000 books, including eleven New York Times bestsellers. She works with publishers, agents, and authors to develop books that are both entertaining and memorable. Connect with Alice at alicesullivan.com.

Q&A
JUDAH SMITH

—

The word *father* means different things to different people. Based on our experiences, *father* can stir a spectrum of emotions and reactions. Some say we live in a fatherless generation, where many grow up with their father figure absent, either figuratively or literally. What is certain is, whatever connotations it brings with it, *father* is a powerful word. The concept of "God the Father" brings with it many questions. If God is our Father, how does that shape our relationship with Him? And how does He react to us? Judah Smith, pastor of the City Church in Seattle, and one of the world's great communicators about Jesus, spoke to us about fathers and how embracing God as our Father changes everything.

Photography: Evan Rummel

"The simplicity is that God answers prayer. Stuff actually happens when you talk to God."

CD: Fathers have such an important role in helping to shape their kids' perspectives of their Father in heaven. How did your dad model a healthy relationship with the Father? How did he keep it enjoyable?

JS: He was so candid. That's the most practical word I can give. I think my dad showed me that a relationship with God was not limited to or defined by a church gathering or a church service or a church function. God is the God of the whole earth, and the earth is His and the fullness thereof, and so I never thought my dad bought in to the idea of that sharp distinction we're prone to make between "Christian" and "non-Christian," meaning Christian music, Christian clothes, Christian cars, Christian food, Christian trees. It gets to the point when you ask, is it all the Lord's—is it all His? Obviously within His beautiful guidelines of Scripture it's to be enjoyed, so my dad and me, we enjoyed sport, we enjoyed good food, we enjoyed good entertainment, we enjoyed good friendships and beautiful places in the world.

As I got a little bit older, we were able to travel a lot as dad was traveling and speaking. I watched my dad enjoy God and enjoy His creation—enjoy all the elements of life in a healthy way.

Someone asked me years ago, "Why didn't you rebel? Was it because you didn't have that classic pastor's kid thing of 'go and discover the meaning of life'?"

I guess my response was, "What would I rebel from?" We were having a blast; we were living the dream, living the adventure of life. God was big; we had to enjoy and laugh and love; and my dad later became not only my dad, but also one of my best friends. For me, that's as practical as Dad skipping Sunday as a preacher to come to Las Vegas and watch me in a basketball tournament. It's a defining moment as a son where you are like, "Wow!" That's a picture of what God the Father is like. God the Father cares about me in Las Vegas playing in a basketball tournament. That matters to Him. It's not just sermons and

songs on a Sunday. That's kind of shaped my worldview and obviously, my view of God.

CD: Going back to what you said in your book *Jesus Is___*, "Acceptance leads to obedience," your dad accepted you no matter what and you naturally wanted to be obedient because of that. You didn't feel you needed to rebel, because you knew you had the acceptance of your father.

JS: There are always moments of "I have to" in life, but my life was more defined by "I get to" and "I want to." I think somewhere in there is the beauty of grace and the beauty of the gospel and the heart-change and the life-change Jesus offers. He doesn't offer a to-do list. He offers the power to transform your desires.

I don't feel like I was raised under the "have to." I was raised under the "isn't this amazing? I'm so loved; I'm so accepted. I get to. I want to. I want to honor my dad. I want to please my dad."

CD: You've mentioned your mom's life message was prayer. You grew up watching her, and your dad as well, in terms of prayer, but what has she taught you about this conversation with God?

JS: Well, recently I've been thinking a lot about prayer. It's not a pure answer to your question, but there's a journey in prayer. First and foremost my mom and dad taught me—particularly my dad. He prayed hours a day, probably a couple of hours a day, as did my mom, so obviously I would see them praying, so those were defining moments and snapshots that are just stuck in there.

The simplicity is that God answers prayer. Stuff actually happens when you talk to God. So I bought in to that pretty early. I've learned to pray about anything and everything, even sports teams—I'm not sure if that's in God's economy—but I think if I care about it, then God cares about it, so I'll talk to Him about it.

Recently I was reading in the gospels, and I was looking at Jesus going extra lengths to talk to the Father. I thought to myself, *Why is it Jesus is praying?* You grow up thinking about praying to get stuff from God, but I'm starting to think Jesus didn't need anything. He was, of course, dependent on the Father, but why did Jesus pray?

I think the primary reason Jesus prayed is because He wanted to be with the Father. I think prayer is not really about getting stuff from God, but getting more of God Himself. Prayer is, I think, to engage with God. It's growing a romance with God, to fall in love with God. That's what moves me to prayer. I don't even know what I want anymore, as silly as that sounds. The further you journey with God, you're like, "Do I really want money?" Is that really the object?

Do I want more square footage in my house? Do I need another house? Do I want to go on another vacation? You might pray like this, but then I start thinking, *God, do you have something better? So scratch that—just give me what you want to give me.* Prayer isn't just getting what I want; it's really about just connecting with God, getting more of Him, and growing. Growing in the knowledge and the grace of Jesus.

CD: How was your prayer life affected by what you went through with your father? Before and after he went up to heaven?

JS: First of all, I never regretted it. I prayed and prayed over everything. I see in Scripture about praying for divine healing. I believe in that more now than ever before. I believe that God is a healer. I've never seen once when Jesus was asked to heal where He said no. So I take that as a pretty good say-so—He wants to heal people.

I never regret all the prayers we prayed for six years that my dad would be healed and be cancer-free; but at the same time you've got to take a step back and go, "Okay, Dad's gone." He wasn't healed. He is now healed and whole for all eternity with Jesus, and I'll be with him before I even know it, right? But there is something much bigger at play than just my dad's body being healthy so he can live twenty-five more years on the earth.

Every time I went to God to talk about my earthly dad, I learned more about God and my relationship grew with God; and maybe that's of even more importance than my dad getting a couple more decades on earth.

In the grand scheme of things in knowing God and loving God, it makes temporary healthy bodies pale in comparison it's so small. It's given me a perspective. I've also learned through the pain. I don't wish it upon anyone; I don't believe that God's a cancer-giver, or God is for cancer. I believe that God is a healer and we live in a fallen world where there are diseases and horrible things, but what's so amazing about God is, He takes the evil—the devil himself, who aims to destroy us and derail us—and He turns it for good, and that is the beauty of what God does. That's certainly happened in my life.

CD: What is prayer? And what is it not?

JS: The metaphor I use—and American culture is steeped in this; I'm not saying it's bad—but I use the metaphor of Santa Claus. Prayer is, for a lot of people, like making a list for Santa. It's like, "Here's the things I want. Oh, and by the way, the reason why I'm anticipating that Santa will get these for me is because I'm on the NICE LIST and not on the NAUGHTY LIST." So prayer becomes a lot of things it's not, if we're not careful. Prayer becomes more of a business transaction as opposed to a conversation, with two people intending on growing a relationship.

The picture I have of prayer is like Luke 15 and the prodigal son story, where the father ran to him and embraced him; I see prayer more as a hug than this kneeling appeal. It's God—I just need to snuggle in here and hold on to you, like Paul wrote: "I'm thinking about you and I'm thanking God for you." Paul is just holding on to God, and he's thanking God, asking God, listening to God, all of which means, "Get God, just hold on to God, and grow in this passionate relationship."

Life is so painful sometimes, it's so mysterious, it's so misleading. I don't need

a Santa Claus list. I need to hold on to God, and I need to feel Him holding on to me. This has to be real. That motivates me. That motivates me to engage with God because I actually want more of God. There is a God, and I can know Him. I want all of Him that I can have. Prayer seems to be one of the primary means by which I can get more of Him.

CD: What do you think the biggest misconception of the gospel is among Christians and how does that impact your conversation with the Father?

JS: There are two things inside me raising their hands, saying, "Pick me! Pick me! Pick me!" Somewhere between believing God's love and accepting His finished work.

I think it's believing that Christianity—or following Jesus—is not predicated upon works and performance. It's based on Jesus' performance, and accepting that. You only believe that when you really, really wade into how profound God's love is for you. I've been wooed by the God of the ages, who has overwhelmed my mind and my heart. I love Him so much that I'm not focusing on morals, ethics, devotion, discipline, my Bible-reading plan, my prayer time, my tithing, or my church attendance. That isn't the focus. All of that happening is part of a romance—of Him! I'm in love with Him!

His love is so expansive. It is so good that it is hard to accept, but I think the biggest misconception is that God's love is like man's love. To be a Jesus follower, like anything else in our fallen world, you have to have perfect attendance, perfect adherence, and only then are you in—otherwise, you're out. No wonder people are like, "Religion is not for me." That's not for me either! I can't do that! We are a band of pardoned rebels—that's what we are.

We are broken people like Humpty Dumpty, who fell off a wall and God put us together again. That's our story. We just have to get the message out. If He loves you today, it proves He'll always love you.

CD: Do you think it's okay to complain to God in prayer?

JS: If King David were sitting here, he'd certainly make a very strong case that a lot of prayers should be complaining and bearing your heart. I think the question needs to be asked in any intimate relationship: Don't we share our deepest, darkest concerns and conversations? If our prayer hasn't got a lot of that going on, I'm not sure if we're being honest with ourselves or honest with God. I certainly offer my fair share of concerns and complaints to God.

CD: Why do you think Jesus prayed to God, even though He was God? You touched on this earlier. Do you think it was just to be closer to the Father?

JS: Somewhere in prayer, He needed friendship and a relationship with the Father. He needed that connection to the Father, and we see how profound that connection was when He was on the cross. "My God, My God, Why have you forsaken me?" He lost that connection, which for Him was obviously life itself. That motivates me. That's my motivation for prayer. It's one of the primary means of getting more of God, and on any day of the week, I'm in.

CD: Do you think Jesus cried, "My God, My God, Why have you forsaken me?" because He no longer felt the connection with the Father, because He was carrying the brunt of all sin?

JS: I think the answer changed the course of human history. He said, "Why have you forsaken me?" And I think the answer based on Scripture is "so I can accept them. I have rejected you, so I can accept them," and Jesus, according to [2 Cor 5:21], became sin so that we might become the righteousness of God. He *had become sin*. A lot of people were crucified. Thousands of people were crucified in Jesus' day. It's important to understand that it wasn't just a crucifixion; Jesus became sin, and He took upon Himself the agony, the terror, the judgment of all of God's justice, the wrath toward all of the error of humanity that ever happened.

All sin—all who will ever sin—was placed upon Jesus, and He literally became sin personified. So the Father turned His face, and there was broken communication between the Father and the Son for the first—and last—time, so that we could now come into the equation. That's how assured we are. We are accepted, we are His.

He rejected his Son so that we would become accepted, and I am now seated with Christ in heavenly places. There's not better news anywhere in the world. What's better than that? It's as free as it gets; all I need to do is accept and receive.

CD: In a message, you said, "Dependence means needing Him, then knowing Him, then becoming more like Him." Does experiencing Jesus daily start with a dependency on Jesus?

"He lost that connection, which for Him was obviously life itself. That motivates me. That's my motivation for prayer. It's one of the primary means of getting more of God, and on any day of the week, I'm in."

JS: I love that scripture: "When I am weak, then I am strong." The power of Christ upon me, I think maybe we've missed that. I think we wallow in our weakness, and we feel like weakness is something to be kept in secret, to not let anybody see. We live in a culture that is obsessed with the strong. Strong. Healthy. Beautiful. In shape. Everything has to be strong. The truth is: we're not. We're not photoshopped on magazine covers. We're just real people with dark spaces.

The need we all have is a perfect setup to connect with Jesus. I genuinely need Jesus every day. My dependency is something I am aware of every day. In a weird sort of way, it turns into a gift. "God, I'm so dependent upon you." I find myself closer to Jesus than ever. The more life speeds up, and the more is expected of me, the more I need Him.

Paul says in Ephesians, for the people living in Ephesus, "Pray that the wisdom of the revelation of the knowledge of God be yours." They were living in deplorable situations. Ephesus was a beautiful city, but the conditions were horrible. You could pray that people wouldn't get sick, that they would get a new job—but the one thing he prayed for was that they would know God more. I thought, *Why did you do that?*

Then it dawned on me. If I am not aware of God's activity in my life, and my circumstances improve, I typically don't grow in my God-awareness. I typically go in the opposite direction. Who needs God when life's clicking on all cylinders? Then I realized if I'm not aware of God, and my circumstances decease and worsen, I don't tend to go to God either. I'm riddled with despair and discouragement.

You begin to realize that the most profound gift we can ever receive is just to know God more. I certainly want to grow in my awareness of God. Connecting with Him is super uncomplicated.

CD: We're living in a fatherless generation. How does that shape and color our perceptions of our Father in heaven?

JS: It's really hard for us to accept God as a Father because the term *father*, or *dad*, has so much negative connotation to it in our culture. I think that's why it is so imperative for us to preach the good news, reveling in God's love for us and His heart for humanity.

An epidemic like the fatherlessness in the world reveals the need of the true Spirit of Jesus transforming paradigms and perspectives and human hearts. Unless God breaks through into the human heart, past all that hurt and bitterness, the brokenness, the un-forgiveness that so much of our generation carries because of the absence of a father, I think we're pretty powerless. It has to transcend an argument and a mental ascent engaging people; it has got to be something supernatural and spiritual. That certainly keeps me praying, "God, help them see you because I am an anomaly that I had a dad who was so engaged, so loving, and so caring." That's something I celebrate every day.

My heart breaks for anyone who has been so hurt, so wounded, and so abused by a father, but I am convinced that the Holy Spirit is up to the task. He's going to show the love of the Father to humanity.

CD: Eventually, love breaks through. People can resist and cross their arms, and for a while, it's awkward, but eventually it breaks through.

JS: It's love that is unconditional, which is the John 3:16 love—*agape*. I think it's exclusively God. Agape exclusively belongs to God. I think He only shares agape with His community, the church. We are the hope of the world because we exclusively carry the antidote to a broken humanity: love with no strings.

Sometimes we're the only version of Jesus people will see in their lifetime. God loves bad people. We don't. We're taught if we see a bad person, distance yourself. Nobody would marry the bride that's kicking and screaming coming down the aisle refusing to say the vows, but God does. That's the whole story. God loves us even when we cheat on

Him. That's wild. Can I demonstrate that? Your reputation will be affected. Jesus' was.

He was the friend of sinners. It was not something to sing songs about and celebrate, which we do today—and I do celebrate it. But when it was said toward Him, it was mean. It was a vicious title. They had no idea it would later bless people, but "friend of sinners" was a shod on His character. He was maligned, and He was chastised for His relationships. But what was He doing? He was loving bad people. We have a ways to go, for sure.

CD: You must have had a bit of scrutiny about some of the people you know, and you have associated with, and you're friends with.

JS: You know what's so funny is the inconsistency. Yeah, there are a few people; I'm involved in their space, and I love them, and we talk pretty regularly. It's just that their endeavors, or their weaknesses and failures, were caught by the paparazzi. There are thousands of people in the community that I lead, several of whom I'm involved in their lives—maybe even more so than some of these recognizable public figures—that make horrible, bad decisions all the time, but no one criticizes me for being in their lives, because no paparazzi caught them in their worst moments.

The inconsistency is palatable, and it's hilarious. We're all making horrible decisions and doing horribly bad stuff, but aren't our doors still open to everyone?

CD: Do you have any encouraging testimonies about prayer?

JS: About a week ago, we had a business lady in our church who was praying for a family member who was pronounced dead in a hospital. A week later, her relative is at home and is alive. The testimony is simple: she was dead, and now she's alive.

She literally prayed for a family member, and she was raised from the dead. The doctors cannot believe it. They have no explanation. It's 100 percent miraculous. Her organs rebuilt themselves. She was pronounced dead. Her body was decaying. She went in there and prayed the prayer that we see in Scripture. "Lazarus was raised from the dead, so why can't God raise my cousin?" So she prayed, she came in, and the doctors showed her how the organs were rebuilding themselves. By the way, the cousin didn't know Jesus, and now she does know Jesus and is following Jesus.

Prayer is so powerful (because it is talking to the all-powerful, all-living, all-loving God) that someone was raised from the dead. The ripple effect it is having in the hospital is ridiculous. People are saying she is a healer and she needs to start traveling the country, visiting hospitals and healing people. What they don't know is we aren't healers; we just love to pray about anyone and anything.

Judah Smith

———

Judah Smith is the lead pastor of the City Church in Seattle, Washington. The City Church is a thriving multisite church noted for its cultural relevance, commitment to biblical integrity and faith, and love for Jesus. Judah is known around the United States and the world for his preaching ministry. His fresh, anointed, humorous messages demystify the Bible and make Christianity real. Judah is also the author of New York Times bestselling books, Jesus Is___ and Life is___.

Connect with Judah on IG @judahsmith

CONTEMPLATION

He holds you firmly in place;
He will not let you fall.

He who keeps you will *never take His eyes off you*
and never drift off to sleep.
What a relief! The One who watches over Israel
never leaves for rest or sleep...
From your first breath to the last breath you breathe,
from this day and forever.

PSALM 121:3–4, 8

So, first and foremost, I urge *God's people to pray.* They should
make their requests, petitions, and thanksgivings on behalf
of all humanity. *Teach them* to pray for kings (or anyone
in high places *for that matter)* so that we can lead quiet,
peaceful lives—reverent, godly, *and holy*—all of which is
good and acceptable before the eyes of God our Savior...

1 TIMOTHY 2:1–3

In a world where almost a majority of marriages end in divorce, we have many children who grow up without a father. We have been chosen by God to have Him as our Father. We learn that by faith we are children of God, and Jesus is our brother and friend. Our lives become God's work if we are obedient. We are completely forgiven and greatly loved by God so we can approach our Father confidently in prayer. Through prayer we grow in our knowledge of the Creator.

Think over these questions and talk with your friends about your answers and their responses.

---

1. When have you felt alone and cut off from God? Would it have been helpful to understand how God loves you as His child and completely forgives you for your rebellion?

2. What are the things that cause you to doubt your relationship with God? How does the promise in Deuteronomy 31:6 help you to sort things out with God?

3. Judah Smith says, "Stuff actually happens when you talk to God." Why do you think that many people don't expect to receive answers to their prayers?

4. Judah observed that the lives of his parents were a kind of prayer journey. Why is it so helpful to think of prayer as an engagement rather than an attempt to get stuff from God?

5. How did Judah respond to his father dying from cancer rather than being delivered from the disease? When have you or someone you know gone through the experience of losing someone close to you after praying for healing? Was God gracious in that experience?

6. How can a loving, heavenly Father allow us to go through difficulties and disappointments? Who do you know that has rejoiced in a very difficult situation?

7. What do you think about Judah saying that the heavenly Father needed to forsake Jesus so that our sins could be forgiven? What do you have in your past that only Jesus' death can absolve?

8. How difficult is it for people in our day to follow Jesus' lead to get away from it all and to be quiet with God? What things do you do to get away?

9. In our culture that honors those who are strong individualists, what obstacles do we face in being like Jesus? How does trying to be strong interfere with following Jesus?

10. God demonstrated His *agape* love for us by putting our sin on Jesus. How can we demonstrate an *agape* love for those around us? When have you had real difficulty in exhibiting agape love?

Other Bible references for you to consider:

Psalm 30:4–5
Matthew 21:21–22
Revelation 7:15–17
Matthew 14:23

WHOSE WE ARE

So imitate me, *watch my ways, follow my example,* just
as I, too, *always seek to* imitate the Anointed One

1 CORINTHIANS 11:1

Words: Alice Sullivan / Photography: Andreas Smitz / Stylist: Karin Stefanov

Social media has no doubt revolutionized our lives—the way we communicate with others, share news, find information, and consume entertainment. Constant feeds are available 24/7 to shine a spotlight on our own lives—or at least the parts we're willing to share with the world—and for a few seconds with each post, tweet, tag, or pin, we feel important. We update our statuses and share pictures with hundreds, if not thousands, of people we may not really even know. And then we wait, ego inflating with every "like" or reply, or shrinking if no one takes notice of our electronic essence.

The problem is—it's not really us that we're portraying. It's who we want to be.

I'm willing to bet that there have been trends, leaders, and followers from the very beginning of humanity. There weren't blogs in biblical times, but there were town meetings and places where people gathered to share news, reminisce about the old, and contemplate the new. It's in these groups that people either felt accepted or rejected based on who they were, what they owned, and what they believed. Being unique was looked upon as something good only if it highlighted a particular strength that benefitted the masses. Stand out too much, and you'll be ridiculed.

When you think about it, we haven't evolved much at all. Our fight for individuality starts as toddlers—as soon as we're able to point to the shirt we want to wear, or sooner if one of our first words was *no*. Somewhere around kindergarten, conformity starts to set in. We want the same backpack as our classmate, Jessica. We want to eat peanut butter and jelly because that's what little Joey brings every day and his sandwich looks so much better than our turkey and cheese.

It seems harmless enough, but these are the first blushes of envy, of a feeling that what we have isn't good enough.

As we grow, so do our wants and needs, as well as our multitude of options, role models, and opinions. By the time we're in junior high, we've developed our own sense of style, a unique personality, musical tastes, and a mash-up of beliefs based on what we've been taught by family, what we talk about with friends, and what we see on social media.

Now don't get me wrong; all of these options can be very freeing and can promote growth if the message is healthy. But when it isn't—when all we see is proof that in order to be liked, loved, wanted, and popular, we should be doing, wearing, and saying one thing—it can be a damaging path that leads to an empty heart.

If we're completely consumed with finding the next best thing, we'll never make enough time to find out who we really are—or more importantly, *whose* we really are.

See, you have nothing to fear. I, *who made you,* will take you back. I have chosen you, named you as My own.
(Is. 43:1)

"As we grow, so do our wants and needs, as well as our multitude of options, role models, and opinions."

Christians are not immune to peer pressure. In fact, in some ways, I think that people of faith have a heavy load to carry. Living a full and happy life is hard enough. Now add the pressure of living a full life and being an example to everyone you come in contact with, no matter the circumstances, and that gets downright scary at times.

What do you do if you have a bad day? Do you let people see you angry, or do you pretend nothing bothers you?

How do you react to disappointment and tragedy? Do you recite a handful of verses about how God's ways are better than your own, or do you genuinely allow yourself to experience a true range of emotions?

How do you make sure that you're taking time each day to pray, meditate, and talk with God? According to Facebook, your neighbor manages to wake up every morning at 4:30 and pray, read two different devotionals, journal her thoughts, and still get to work on time. You, on the other hand, hit snooze three times every morning and are lucky to brush your hair and make it to work wearing matching socks. How in the world does she do it? What does she have that you don't?

And does posting pretty Bible verses on Instagram count as devotional time? (I'm asking for a friend.)

Just like skinny jeans and tattoos won't make you more relevant in a fashion-crazed society, trying to emulate other Christians by repeating their actions and language, copying their personal style, and buying the latest Bible journaling accessories won't make you any more effective in reaching the world for Jesus.

The world doesn't need another poser. What it needs is just one authentic *you*.

For we are the product of His hand, *heaven's poetry etched on lives,* created in the Anointed, Jesus, to accomplish the good works God arranged long ago. (Eph. 2:10)

Great! That sounds like a breath of fresh air, both a relief and a release to be yourself, right? But what exactly does that mean—being *authentic*?

By definition, it means "real, true, based on fact, and made to look like an original."

In relationships, that means being honest, open with our feelings, forming our own opinions based off our experiences, and being supportive of others who might even be different from us.

In fashion, that means rockin' whatever style of clothes you feel comfortable wearing that fits your personality and makes you feel great, regardless of the cost or the brand.

In our personal faith walk, that means learning how we best communicate with God, discovering what our strengths are, accepting our weaknesses, and moving forward, growing in ways that only we can grow.

I've never had a hard time expressing myself through the way I dress and communicate, and I'm thankful that I've become pretty comfortable in my own skin. But I've always struggled with developing and maintaining a consistent conversation with God. It sounds so simple but feels so difficult.

I tried getting up early, reading my devotional, and praying for a set amount of time each morning. And it worked great for two or three days until I either slept in or had an early work deadline that threw my whole day's timeline off.

So I tried taking breaks during the day to meditate and talk to God about all the things I was thankful for and all the things I was concerned about. And again, that worked for a few days until I forgot to do it. Finally, I figured it out: if I didn't get up early enough to journal every day and I forgot to take breaks to meditate, surely I'll have time and remember to pray every night before I go to bed.

Except that didn't last long either.

I failed at waking up early and devoting time to God. I failed at taking breaks each day to talk with God. And I couldn't remember to pray every night before bed. In my mind, that made me a huge failure—a lazy Christian. Thousands of other people appear to have these amazing prayer lives; they receive life-changing revelations at 5:00 a.m. when I'm still sleeping. They have a daily schedule they follow and let nothing stand in the way of their quiet time. They actually fill up their prayer journals in a multitude of colorful inks and have to buy new ones while I just rearrange mine on my bedside table so *it looks like* I've used them all recently. Why couldn't I be more like them? What's wrong with me?

Ouch.

It took longer than it should have for me to realize that *nothing* is wrong with me. While I was too focused on trying to mimic someone else's life, I had managed to overlook the undeniable positives of my own faith journey. Sure, I may not get up early every morning and read my devotional and write in my journal when scheduled, but I do talk to God throughout the day, even if it is pausing for a few seconds to be thankful for what I do have. I don't fill my Twitter feed with Bible verses, but I always try to encourage others and see the best in people. While I'm always careful to not hurt feelings, I'm not afraid to speak my mind and offer sound advice; my friends have always told me they value that about me.

Maybe I wasn't meant to be a hard-and-fast rule-follower after all. Maybe you weren't either. Maybe I am meant to do exactly what I am doing—living and loving as only I can.

So here's to embracing your strengths, whatever they may be. Learn to be courageous. Focus on the positives. However you feel fulfilled and renewed, however you communicate with God, however you show the love of Christ to those around you—let it be authentically and unashamedly your own brand of heaven on earth.

Since you are all set apart by God, made holy and dearly loved, clothe yourselves with *a holy way of life*: compassion, kindness, humility, gentleness, and patience. Put up with one another. Forgive. Pardon any offenses against one another, as the Lord has pardoned you, because you should act in kind. But above all these, put on love! Love is the perfect tie to bind these together. (Col. 3:12–14)

Q&A
CHARLOTTE GAMBILL

——

Jesus told Simon Peter and Andrew "follow me." He extends the same invitation to us. But what does it mean to be a follower of Christ? Charlotte Gambill (Life Church in England) has been learning about what this means since age fourteen when she dedicated her life to serving Christ and following Him. From there, she has been taken on a journey to become a church leader, overseeing multiple campuses across Europe with her husband Steve, an author and world-renowned speaker, all the while following Christ and His will for her life. Charlotte shared some of what she's learned about what it means to be a follower of Christ.

Photography: Hannah Burton
Stylist: Nathan Klein / Make-up: Ami Cassidy

"God wants to instruct
us all in the rhythm
He has designed
for our destiny."

CD: Do you have an illustration from your early life where it would have been easy to follow the crowd that would have led you to a very different place than where you are now? What kept you from following the crowd?

CG: At the age of fourteen, I knew God was drawing my heart toward some kind of ministry. I did not know what this would look like, but the best way I can describe it was that I suddenly had an appetite to be around God's house and learn His Word. I was hungry for more of Him.

This was something that was not shared by my immediate circle of friends at the time. They wanted to do what all the other fourteen-year-olds were doing, hanging out, going to the movies, and there was nothing wrong with that but for me a change was taking place. I became aware that I was going to have to decide who I was going to follow: my friends, peer pressure or this sense of call I knew was on me.

It made for some hard conversations. Friends who did not get my choices felt I was ignoring them, and there were those who thought I was becoming boring and God-obsessed. It was hard at such a young age to feel I was going against the crowd, but God reminded me of Timothy's life. When Timothy's mentor Paul spoke to him about his future, he told him to devote himself to the reading of Scripture and to knowing the Word.

No one can be devoted for you, and following will require you to make some calls that can be costly but if it is worth possessing, then it is worth paying.

CD: How do you distinguish between a Christian who is a fan of Jesus and one who is a follower?

CG: Fans come for the show, followers come to serve. Fans are about the main stage, followers are happy backstage. Fans are part of a club, followers are part of a cause. Fans want a moment of connection, followers want a lifetime of dedication. Fans leave when the lights go out, followers stay when everyone else has gone home. Jesus fans know of Him, Jesus followers are willing to be known by Him.

CD: In a culture where comfort, convenience, and speed are so important, what can we do to become followers who can endure discomfort, inconvenience, and waiting patiently for God's timing?

CG: We all have to deal with the challenge of self over surrender. It's our selfishness that asks for things to be easier, faster, and so on. Our culture is geared to be self-serving, and it tells us to put ourselves first and fight for what is ours. Yet to be a true follower, the Bible says we have to learn how to put surrender before self, which is countercultural.

If Jesus said in Matthew 20:28, "I have come not to be served but to serve," then how much more do we need to learn to embrace that model? If you are struggling to be patient or to endure, then my suggestion is to move your attention away from what you are seeking or feel you need and instead place your attention on the needs of others.

It's our awareness of the bigger picture that helps us gain the right perspective in every circumstance. When we realize how much He has already done for us, we can rest in what He will yet do. And when we realize how much we already have, we stop stressing over what we don't yet have.

Don't let self determine how you serve. Don't let impatience limit your options; let trust and surrender become core values, and you will find that your following will remain faithful to God's timing.

CD: How is your experience of Jesus impacted by how you follow Him?

CG: The more I know Him, the more I want to follow Him. It is my increasing knowledge of Jesus that has deepened my ability and desire to be His follower. The more I spend time in His Word, in worship, the more attuned I become to the path He wants me to follow.

In the Bible, it says in Galatians 5:25, "Keep in step with the spirit," which suggests we can also be out of step. I believe the more I choose to be in His presence and around His promises, the more I am in His Word and planted in His house—the more I understand the way I should respond, where He wants to lead and how He wants to use me.

CD: Is it possible to be a follower of Jesus in one area of life but not in another?

CG: Of course, I think we can be selective followers. Often when we first come to know Jesus, we place our life to follow His lead closely; but the more we travel in our journey as believers, the more traffic we add to the lanes of our life and the less purposeful we can be in following.

At times we can be strong, following His word in one area of our life, but totally unconnected and undisciplined in another area. We can be focused in our faith in one lane and distracted by other things that call for our attention in another. You can follow Jesus on Sundays in church, but on Monday you can switch lanes and follow the demands and agendas around you. You can follow Jesus with your serving but not be a follower in your giving. It's a journey we all are on. We have to look at our lives in every season and check that we are not drifting where we once were following.

CD: Do people ever question whether your level of sacrifice is too high for a follower of Jesus?

CG: I often get asked if it is right that I leave my family to preach and travel. This is something I have had to personally bottom out with every season of life; but because I know that God loves my family more than I ever could, I look for my pace in life to find His peace.

I believe we all have a rhythm for our lives. If God is our partner in this great dance, then He has a tempo for each of us to dance with Him. God's calling on all our lives will have a cost, but He will never lay anything on you that is too heavy for you to bear; so the problem often is not that we have too much to carry, but that we don't know how to carry it.

God wants to instruct us all in the rhythm He has designed for our destiny. Some people are graced for a faster tempo than others; therefore, when people may look at my life as a wife, mom, or minister and ask how can I do all that, I say, "I am not doing it all alone."

I have to keep making sure I am not just working for God but that I am working with God; if I am working with Him, then the rhythm will be right—not just for me but for those I carry with me.

CD: We know we enter into a relationship with Jesus freely, but does that mean we often don't realize we have to actively build that

relationship, or sometimes not even recognize that there is more that we can experience?

CG: I am sure we can all settle at times in our following. We can go into autopilot mode in our relationship, where we disengage from that small voice that often nudges us in a different direction or quietly whispers instruction to our hearts.

We are called to be co-workers with God, and we have an active part to play; He did not just save you, but He called you.

I suggest that if your life is predictable, or what you are building becomes monotonous or boring, then you may need to press refresh on your journey with God. Jesus didn't call us into a safe life; He called us into a life of adventure, where we would be commissioned and sent out to be His light in the dark and His voice for the voiceless.

The way to recognize if you have lost that connection somewhere is to look for where comfort has replaced cause, and if that's you, just sign up afresh today and recommit to the greatest adventure of all. His great commission.

CD: What have you learned over the years following Jesus about the kind of relationship He wants with you and how have you actively developed it?

CG: That's just it: He wants a relationship with you, and it is as personal and unique as you are. We need to understand we are not called into religion but into relationship; and just like any great relationship, it thrives with time, trust, investment, love, and grace.

I have found that God wants me to be all He created me to be. He wants a relationship where I believe what He speaks over me, where I enjoy the journey rather than endure it.

I know some people may say that we have to have a set way to pray and approach God, but honestly I think my relationship with God is a lot less complicated than that. Just like my relationships with my closest friends, they work because I am choosing to make them work.

It says in John 15:16 that "we didn't choose God first but He first chose us as friends," which blows my mind. This truth delivers you and me from trying to impress God or strive for this relationship.

I develop my relationship with Jesus like I would with a friend. I spend time with Him; I involve Him in my everyday life; I learn about His ways and embrace His wisdom for my life.

Your relationship with God can be as rich and rewarding as you decide to make it.

CD: How do you keep a sense of wonder and expectancy, and is it harder to stay a follower when you are a success?

CG: First of all, I don't see what I am doing as a success; I see it as obedience. I simply keep saying yes to God, and that leads me on some pretty crazy adventures. I think that's where many get confused; we overcomplicate what it means to be a follower. I think we lose our sense of wonder because we have a false sense of what success is, so we stop seeing the wonder in front of us because we think it must be something that we are yet to attain.

I think we need to stop letting other people's supposed success determine our own levels of satisfaction and expectation.

Every day I am fully expectant for God to do incredible things. Every day I am fully aware of His mighty hand and awesome provision. Every day, even in test and trial, I am in awe that He would help and love me.

CD: What are the trappings you've most commonly seen that prevent new Christians from going on to develop an authentic relationship with Jesus?

CG: Religion, legalism, a sense of people feeling they are less than. Too often we forget that we were once one of those new believers, and just like a newly born baby we need to handle those who are new with great care.

They need a lot of love, a lot of patience, and a lot of family to help them grow and thrive; but too often we greet new believers with a lot of information, expectation, and intimidation. We need to help those who are taking their first steps to find their feet.

The best way to introduce someone to Jesus is to show them how He loves, cares, and wants them to succeed. Once they know Him as their Father, they will find it easier to learn how to be His followers.

Charlotte Gambill

———

Charlotte Gambill is a church leader, author, and international speaker and is lead pastor with her husband, Steve, at Life Church, United Kingdom. Charlotte has an infectious love for life, a deep love for people, and zealous love for God's house. Her passion is to build the local church across the earth, to see people reach their full potential, and to develop and strengthen leadership. Charlotte lives in the north of England with her husband and their two children, Hope Cherish and Noah Brave.

Connect with Charlotte at charlottegambill.com and on IG @charlgambill

CONTEMPLATION

Brothers and sisters, in light of *all I have shared with you about* God's mercies,
I urge you to offer your bodies as a living and holy sacrifice *to God,* a sacred
offering that brings Him pleasure; this is your reasonable, essential worship. Do
not allow this world to mold you in its own image. Instead, be transformed *from
the inside out* by renewing your mind. As a result, you will be able to discern
what God wills and whatever God finds good, pleasing, and complete.

ROMANS 12:1–2

He gave His body for our sakes and will not only break us free from *the chains of* wickedness, but He will also prepare a community uncorrupted by the world that He would call His own—people who are passionate about doing the right thing.

TITUS 2:14

Living in a society where being the very best (even though we are trying to be just like everyone else) is admired, it is increasingly more taxing to try to imitate Jesus. Although there is a growing need to have the best things and to appear to be better than all others, there is increasing pressure to fit in with others. The Christian's walk of faith is not about fitting in with others or having more or better things than others. We are called to serve as our Lord served. We are called to an obedient faith and to live a holy life. Neither of these is greatly valued in our society.

The following questions and Scripture references are designed to help you apply this chapter to your life. Discuss your thoughts with friends as you move further along your walk with Jesus.

1. How can believers stand out against the backdrop of an amoral culture and yet avoid calling attention to themselves as being self-centered or self-absorbed?

2. How is who we are as followers of Jesus any different than our abilities or our accomplishments?

3. How can our pursuit of a "full and happy life" keep us from enjoying the life we now have? What do you think the secret of a full Christian life is?

4. Why is it so difficult for many Christians to live a transparent life, being open and honest about their personal struggles and obstacles to spiritual growth?

5. How can we avoid falling into the spiritual laziness trap that many believers experience? What can we do to experience fresh and meaningful ongoing communication with God?

6. What are the things that have drawn you closer to God in your spiritual journey, and what are the things that have pushed you further away from God?

7. Charlotte Gambill describes some of those she has ministered to as either fans of Jesus or as followers of Jesus. What are the characteristics of those in each category? Tell of a time when you were a fan and another time when you were a follower?

8. Charlotte speaks of being either self-serving or trusting and surrendering. Are there times when these two positions are similar? What are the characteristics of someone who is trusting and surrendering to God?

9. Charlotte sees her personal success as being a product of obedience rather than her achievement. How can working hard and being successful be an act of disobedience? How can focusing on obedience lead to personal success?

10. What aspect of your life do you think makes it difficult for you to trust God and experience a devoted, full, successful spiritual existence?

Other Bible references for you to consider:

Acts 20:20–24
2 Thessalonians 3:7–13
James 5:9–11
1 Peter 4:1–2

LIVING FROM A PLACE OF REST

Come to Me, all who are weary and burdened, and I will give you rest. Put My yoke upon your shoulders—*it might appear heavy at first, but it is perfectly fitted to your curves.* Learn from Me, for I am gentle and humble of heart. *When you are yoked to Me,* your weary souls will find rest. For My yoke is easy, and My burden is light.

MATTHEW 11:28–30

Words: Biju Thampy / Photography: Vlad Vasylkevych

"Instead of spending every waking moment being 'productive,' what if we said no to the things we don't *need* to do, and yes to only the things we are *called* to do."

I work in a place of tremendous need. Mumbai, the financial hub of India, is also the melting pot of different cultures. Despite these glamorous titles given to our city, the streets of Mumbai are populated with hundreds of homeless children. Children are abandoned and left to fend for themselves. More often than not, they ultimately get sucked into a vortex of slavery, exploitation, and injustice. These children, if left abandoned and unreached, can go down nameless and voiceless in history.

In addition to the staggering numbers of abandoned children, India has close to 400,000 villages that are unreached for Christ.

As you can see, the need is massive and the magnitude of the problem is overwhelming. Responding to the need with our own strength and our own power can leave us feeling worn out and completely washed out. I know, because it happened to me.

When I was thirty-four years old, I came to a point of total exhaustion in the midst of a hectic schedule of ministering across India. I had such a burning passion for my nation that I would travel great distances in all kinds of vehicles just to get to my destination to share the good news of the gospel.

While it was exhilarating work, it was also draining. I experienced such physical fatigue and my body was in such bad shape that when I finally went to a doctor, she said that if I were a dog, she would have me put down.

On that day, I realized I couldn't do all of what I wanted to do *in my own strength*.

To be honest, I didn't have much strength left. I still had the passion and the drive, but I would have to change my level of activity in order to reduce the damage I was inflicting on my body. I would need to learn to work out of rest so I didn't work myself to death.

The Christian life is not about us trying to live for God, because we really can't measure up to His standards; rather it is about God living through us. Christian ministry is not what we do for God—it is what God does in and through us. But if we are so busy all the time with doing what *we want to do*—even with the things we feel are important or necessary—are we really letting God live, speak, or move through us?

Instead of spending every waking moment being "productive", what if we said no to the things we don't *need* to do, and yes to only the things we are *called* to do. I imagine we'd see our productivity increase and our stress and activity levels decrease, and we'd encounter a sense of peace we've long forgotten about.

> But as for me, I will look to the Eternal One, and my hope is in the True God who will save me. My God will hear me. (Mic. 7:7)

Living with this premise in mind—working from rest and allowing the Holy Spirit to guide our time—helps us to accomplish so much more. Working out of rest requires us to be totally dependent on the

Holy Spirit. We can't do everything—nor should we—but we can accomplish what He wants us to do.

I now realize I cannot do a thing without the Holy Spirit. When I consult with Him first each day, I am amazed at how my work seems to prioritize itself.

We see the best example of this daily prioritizing in the life of Jesus Himself. In Matthew 11:30, He said, "My yoke is easy, and my burden is light."

We can't set the world straight in our own strength, nor can we attempt to tell the world how good we are. These are just recipes for struggle and turmoil. Instead, we have to allow Jesus to live through us and show Himself to the world, for only He is truly good.

We don't need to show the world how able or efficient we are, either. Instead, we should allow Jesus to show the world the power of His resurrected life in and through us. That way, the burden is not on us to prove *ourselves*. All we have to do is hand over the reins to Jesus, who so powerfully works through us.

What is the reward in all of this? Well, it's joy! The joy that comes from us being used by Him and for Him. We also inherit a great deal of peace once we realize the world is not only ours to fix.

> If they hear and *choose to* serve Him,
>   then they end their days in prosperity
>   and their years in felicity. (Job 36:11)

As a child, I remember growing up in our family home, always surrounded by people whom my parents helped and ministered to. On many occasions, there were threats on my parents' lives because of the work they did for the Lord. As a result, my siblings and I had to stay confined at home many times or had to move around with supervision. In spite of that, what I remember most is the feeling of joy that we had as a family.

Years later, I was with a couple of my friends, evangelizing in India, when we fell victim to an angry mob. We managed to escape, but not before one of our friends was attacked quite viciously and his shirt torn.

As we made our getaway in a taxi, this friend stopped the taxi driver and said he wanted to go back to the scene of the attack. We were all shocked and asked him why on earth he would want to do that, to which he replied, much to our amusement, "I need to find my shirt buttons."

The attack had only damaged his clothing; it hadn't even put so much as a scratch in his unwavering commitment to God.

Serving Christ is a joyful experience. Our motivation is only that every man and woman should hear the good news. It's too good not to share! All of this and more can be done if we work out of rest.

Working out of rest helps us to go the extra mile with His strength propelling us forward. Working with Jesus helps us to enjoy the journey. This journey is not free of burdens or difficulties, but in the midst of it all, He gives us His peace and joy.

Working out of rest also helps us to think clearly, since God downloads His thoughts for humanity directly into our spirit.

> I want you to know that the Eternal your God is *the only true* God. He's the faithful God who keeps His covenants and shows loyal love for a thousand generations to those who *in return* love Him and keep His commands. (Deut. 7:9)

Working out of rest also makes it easy for others to work with us. When we work out of strife and struggle, as a leader especially, we become cranky and upset with those around us. That's not something God wants for us. Instead, when we work from a place of rest, people gravitate toward us and want to work with us and fill up the gaps in our lives.

Ultimately, this is God's plan for our lives. Every believer will experience such joy and fulfillment when he learns to be dependent entirely on the Holy Spirit and work out of rest.

Jesus says to His disciples in John 15:5, "Without Me, you will accomplish nothing"

He says this in context of Jesus being the vine and we the branches. If we look at it closer, we understand that the purpose of the branch is to bear fruit. But the branch doesn't have to struggle and strive to bear this fruit. All it has to do is totally depend on the vine and draw its essence and nourishment from it. When it does, fruit is the natural by-product produced.

Biju Thampy

Biju Thampy is the founder and president of Vision Rescue (visionrescue.co.in), a charitable society catering to the needs of the street children, feeding and giving them non-formal education. Vision Rescue is involved in counseling, rehabilitating, guiding, and giving medical attention to the needy, deprived, addicted, and abused on the streets.
Biju is director of Missions of New India Church of God, an indigenous nonprofit organization, which includes over 3,600 churches, sixteen Bible training centers, six children's homes, schools, vocational and skill training centers, a rehabilitation center, refugee homes, six mobile evangelistic teams, and street children's programs.
He lives in Mumbai, India, with his wife, Secunda, and their three boys, Timothy, Nathan, and Benjamin. He is the senior pastor of the Gateway Church in Mumbai.

Connect with Biju on IG @bijuthampy

Q&A
GARY CLARKE

—

When we become Christians we become disciples of Jesus. But what does that mean? How can we be teachable so that we move forward into a deeper relationship with Him? We spoke to Pastor Gary Clarke, lead pastor of Hillsong Church London, about learning and growing in our understanding of what God has called us to do and who He wants us to be.

Photography: Vlad Vasylkevych & Kateryna Seleznova

CD: As you grew up, who were the people who influenced you the most in learning?

GC: Probably one of the biggest lessons I had growing up was when I first started playing cricket. I hated the first game, and I never knew the game could be so boring. I went back the second week, and I felt like giving up and not coming back.

I remember my mother saying, "You can't stop playing cricket until the end of the season. You started, so you will finish."

I must have been about eight or nine years old. I finished the whole season playing cricket—I hated it—but I had learned to do the things I didn't like doing. My parents were like that. If you do something, you see it through; you don't have a bailout clause. You look to do it the best you can, even if you don't like it.

CD: Is that something that's shaped your life?

GC: I just believe that you have to be able to do the things you don't like doing with the same amount of energy as the things you do like doing. Very little of life is about doing what you like doing. You need to learn how to do what you don't like doing, and learn how to do it well. Everything you do opens the door to the next thing. Not everything is necessarily a stepping-stone—not everything is a door of opportunity; but life does build precept upon precept and line upon line.

I believe that what you're doing now, and how you're doing what you're doing now, will determine the next step, the next opportunity, the next level—all those words we use. *Now* has a great bearing on *next*.

CD: You had a career as a horse trainer. What led you into that, and what did you learn from it?

GC: I was about twenty-three, and I had quite a few staff—way too many for a person of that age—so there was responsibility. I wasn't really that good at it.

I learned some lessons. One of them was that I had made a mistake—a fairly significant mistake—that had cost the boss thousands. I went and told him, and he said, "Oh, well, that's life."

I was freaked out. A little bit after that, I was called into his office because I had gone out to purchase some things for what we needed, and instead of paying $5.50 for them, I paid

$6, which wasted 50¢ per item because it was just easier to buy the more expensive items.

When I went into his office, he blew me apart, for what seemed to be a small amount of money to me. I thought, *This is ridiculous. A few weeks back, I wasted thousands, and now I've wasted maybe ten dollars, and you're going crazy at me.*

I went back and asked him, "Why did you behave the way you did when it wasn't that much?"

He said to me—and I'll never forget it—that it actually had nothing to do with how much money it was. He said, "It's all got to do with your approach, and that you actually, intentionally, wasted my money. You need to understand—it's *my* money, and you wasted *my* money. The other thing was an accident and couldn't be helped. You intentionally wasted my money, and that's not how you do life."

It's one of those life lessons.

CD: When you became a Christian, what were the first steps you took in becoming a student of Jesus?

GC: When I was horse riding, I always had a teacher and I always had a coach. So I was always in a place where I had to present myself to somebody who would pull apart what I was doing so that I could learn. It wasn't a foreign concept to me to sit down and listen to somebody preaching and to listen to what they were saying. It wasn't a foreign thing for me to look to a pastor and say, "I recognize your authority and I recognize your position. I'm going to listen to what you say, and I'm going to apply it." Because that's how I learned horse riding. Whether I was good at riding or bad at riding is irrelevant. How I learned was, I listened and I actually applied.

The key, I think, is a receptivity that has a respect for authority and a respect for what somebody else has to teach you. Obviously, this applies to Jesus and the Holy Spirit. We can be dismissive, and we can be pious. But how you walk before men is how you walk before God.

I learned most from people.

CD: You once said, your attitude toward your boss is your attitude toward God.

GC: Yes, my attitude toward human authority pretty much reflects my submission to God.

CD: How do you think Jesus modeled teachability to His disciples even though He was God?

GC: It's important that you realize Jesus is both 100 percent man and 100 percent God. So in His humanity, He still had to submit Himself to the Holy Spirit and the heart of the Father. It's almost like the taming of the human spirit, which seeks after its own view and its own independence.

In our core as human beings, we love our own opinion. Jesus—like all of us—would have to put that aside so that it wouldn't flare up and rule.

In His humanity, He demonstrated His submission to the Father.

CD: Even when He was in the garden, Jesus prayed, "Not my will be done, but yours." He still struggled.

GC: Jesus always strived in His humanity for a bigger purpose, which is the purpose of God. It wasn't, *what's in it for me?* It was, *what are the purposes of God that I'm aligning myself to?* If we're going to learn anything, we need to learn how to align ourselves to the purposes of God, as opposed to trying to bring God into our context.

CD: How has God used desert seasons, such as obscurity, to teach you?

GC: I quit ministry once. I think I was out of it for about two years, because I got disillusioned with church leadership, and I got disillusioned with church. I didn't quit church, but I quit ministry.

When I looked at myself, I didn't like who I was becoming, so I made a decision to remove myself and rediscover what God was all about. My biggest lesson was that I had to learn how to trust church leadership again. I probably completely distrusted it and had to consciously make a decision to trust these people.

I think, ultimately, you have to trust people. You can spend your whole life trusting God, never trusting people, but we cannot separate ourselves *from* people.

CD: Do you have any defining moments in your relationship with Jesus that really impacted how you saw Him and experienced Him daily?

GC: There's never really been "a moment," but there have been loads of moments when I have seen the faithfulness of God appear in my daily life.

When I first became a Christian, I made a decision that this is real, this is true—I have just seen the consistent faithfulness of God in life, whether that be internally (in internal issues) or externally (in circumstantial issues).

I have seen the faithfulness of God. I think some of the most impacting things were when I saw my ideals of God become real and tangible.

I saw it firsthand when we prayed for the sick and people were healed. I realized these weren't just ideals; I believed them to be true, and I saw those ideals as realities. I've seen it firsthand—what He does in peoples' lives. I know He has done this in mine.

I can't say there was a moment when I said, "Here it is." I have consistently seen God work both internally and circumstantially. It can't be anything but "this is real."

CD: Do people miss the fact that they actually have to be involved in building the relationship and that it won't just happen? Why do you think that is?

GC: If we're not careful, we can unintentionally turn Jesus into a genie. He's the one who grants us our wishes. He'll grant us the desires of our heart, whatever our desires are. "Jesus, you're going to do it for me." I think it's very easy to turn Him into that, as opposed to a "this is a relationship that sustains me that has an eternal consequence, and not everything's perfect now" type of consequence. It's very easy to do that.

Undeniably, you have to become a person who actually opens his Bible and actually understands the whole picture of what the Bible is about. If we're not careful, people will use it as a book of quotes and try to make it do things and say things. It was never written to be an accurate book of human history. It is the story of God and humanity. You actually have to give of yourself to understand that, because when you understand that, you understand God and humanity. You actually start to understand how He works in you.

If you know how He works in you, you can confidently seek Him when you need Him, or when, perhaps, you have been ignoring Him.

I think it's interesting how Paul said, "Pray without ceasing." That can mean a lot of things, but I think what that means is that you need to live life with a God-consciousness. "I am conscious of you, Lord, wherever you are. Whatever is going on, I know you're in this moment."

At the same time, you need to have some form of ritual to God. However that works for you. I coined a phrase, "Have coffee with God." I get up every morning, sit in a chair, and have coffee with God. I don't know if He likes coffee. There's a habitual side to it. You have to foster it. It's like any relationship. You have to get to Him.

How do you get to know Him? You get to know His ways, which is revealed in His Word. You get to see Him in your life. It's this constant thing.

CD: How do you feel secular culture can infiltrate kingdom culture when it comes to staying planted and being taught by a leader?

GC: Today's culture is shaped by postmodern, secular, pluralist, individualistic, intellectualist, humanist rules. It's woven into today's culture, especially Western culture, and it's shaped by so many of those elements.

We've got to be careful that those views don't seep over into our Christianity. Yes, we are individuals, but we're a part of something. We're actually a part of His church, Christ's body. They're not two separate entities.

"We've got to be careful that those views don't seep into our Christianity."

Paul uses the metaphor of the body to help us understand what church is. Individualism can play a part in that. Intellectualism—"I'm smart in this area, so I'm qualified to be opinionated about something I know nothing about"—we need to be careful of that.

We've got to be careful of humanism when it creeps in, where it's all about *me*.

Secularism is another thing to be aware of, where God can affect this part of my life, but not this part. They're all subtleties that can creep in.

We've got to be aware of the world we live in. There's no point in getting bent out of shape about it. It comes back to "What is my true north?" If truth and morality are relative, then what is my relative? Is it grounded in the Bible? Or am I going to create a "relative" and try to fit the Bible in?

Perhaps I need to create my relative out of the Bible. I've got to be grounded somewhere.

CD: There are absolutes. The Bible says there are absolutes.

GC: We all need absolutes. People say there are no absolutes, but you ask them, "Is that true?" and they say, "Absolutely." We live in a world where we define it. So you have to be careful how you define it, and whether or not it's real.

CD: When people ask you what is their destiny in life, how do you respond?

GC: It's a bit of a controversial question. I do think we spend way too much time thinking "God's got something for me" rather than "I'm for God, so let's see what He does with me." Does He have a destiny for me, and all those sorts of questions—they're irrelevant until you actually pursue God. If your pursuit is God, He's going to direct you and all of those things are going to shape your life.

To believe that I have to live out the eighty or so years of my life, and then I hit a destination—I don't know. I think a lot of people spend their lives trying to find this thing as if it's a secret God's got hidden. God doesn't play hide-and-seek with our lives.

A lot of us have got to get it down to, "Am I submitted in my heart toward God?" Then a lot of these questions people ask go away.

Often, the most confused people are the ones who don't want to lay down their lives. I think when you lay down your life, and it's all about the purpose of God, you stop asking these questions. The questions don't matter. We get all bent out of shape. Is it, "Do I have a plan?" or "Does Jesus have a plan?" Or is

there even a plan? Who knows? It becomes such a complex thing for people because they're chasing after the wrong thing.

Instead, let's say, "I have laid down my life. Here it is, God. I'm a living sacrifice. I'm going to lay down my life because you're going to do this with me, aren't you, God?"

CD: Do you have any favorite stories in the New Testament about the attitudes of the disciples? Is there anything we can learn from them?

GC: I like the story in Mark where Jesus is talking to the disciples. He found them arguing among each other about who was going to be the most famous.

I think about the world today—who is the most famous? It might just be a bigger question than it needs to be. If it were an issue back then, it's probably an issue now. What

fascinated me is how Jesus was surprised by how much it meant to them. It goes back to what we ultimately try to accomplish.

I think the other standout one is in Matthew 9 and into 10. Pray to the Lord of the Harvest to send laborers. We pray *for* laborers. I think Jesus was saying, "Are you prepared to *be* one of the laborers in the harvest?"

CD: There are certain Bible characters who you tend to go back to in your sermons: Daniel, Gideon, the Good Samaritan. What is it about those characters that makes you go back to them? What attracts you to them?

GC: I think they're great examples of "deny yourself, take up your cross, and follow me."

Daniel became an incredible man of influence but remained consistent in his character. Yes, his eyes were on God, but he remained consistent. Gideon had to believe that who he was from God's perspective was more important than how he saw himself from his own perspective.

We can spend way too much time focusing on what's wrong with us rather than on what's right. I think Gideon is a great example of that. Those characters are examples of people who remain consistent and lay hold of God in a way that's powerful.

The Good Samaritan always stands out to me because Jesus was saying, "The neighbor that you're trying to be mindful of is anyone you're in proximity to. Even the ones you don't like." I tried to afford myself the luxury of not liking anybody for too long. You can't let that rule you. You've got to hold yourself accountable. You can't hold things against people for too long. Keep a short memory.

CD: The Great Commission of God: How can we be a part of it? What do you get from that?

GC: We have the responsibility to model Christ to a world that doesn't know Him. That's not modeling by saying, "Here's my perfect life," but by our faith, our trust. If I can talk about Him, I talk about Him in a personal way. If a person asks me about Him, I talk about Him as a person I know, not as a person I know of.

I think every single human being who knows Jesus ought to be a soul-winner. That should be our endeavor. We should be contributing to souls being saved.

The way we play our part in this amazing thing called "the church" is actually vital. We don't try to separate kingdom, body, and church—they're inseparable things. We've all got to play our part, and we've all got something to contribute.

Gary Clarke

———

Gary Clarke is lead pastor of Hillsong Church London, a thriving, growing church with six campuses and thousands gathering every weekend to worship. He moved from Australia to London with his wife, Cathy, and their two children in 1999. As a pastor, teacher, and leader, Gary is passionate about seeing people live to their fullest potential, empowering them to practically reach and impact their day-to-day world. He is devoted to providing real solutions to some of the problems humanity faces, from youth issues in London to the worst of world poverty, and has initiated a variety of partnerships and projects that bring justice to people who find themselves in less-fortunate circumstances.

Connect with Gary on IG @garyjamesclarke

CONTEMPLATION

Listen! The Lord, the Eternal, the Holy One of Israel says,
Eternal One: In returning and rest, you will be saved.
In quietness and trust you will find strength.

ISAIAH 30:15

Since the day we got this good news about you, we have not stopped praying for you. We ask: *Father,* may they clearly know Your will and achieve *the height and depth of* spiritual wisdom and understanding. May their lives be a credit to You, Lord; and *what's more,* may they continue to delight You by doing every good work and growing in the true knowledge that comes from being close to You.

COLOSSIANS 1:9–10

It is natural to want to be liked and respected. Living among Christians, we have the further pressure to be holy. When these add to our desire to serve our Lord, we tend to push too hard and become exhausted. God has provided the concept of Sabbath, or rest, for our relief. He has also made available the power of the Holy Spirit and the fact that Jesus desires to live through us. So why does the spiritual life seem so hard? We struggle to do it all by ourselves. We are not called to be burdened with our walk of faith but to share the joy of our Lord.

Consider the following questions and share your thoughts with friends.

1. Why does it seem that those outside the faith have an easier life than we of faith have? Why do some Christians burn out in the struggle to live as a Christian should? What things cause us to focus on the problems of life rather than on the joy of overcoming?

2. What does it mean for Christ to live within us? What are the obstacles to "Christ within" becoming a reality?

3. Explain the concept of "working out of rest." When have you experienced the sensation of rest while you were in the midst of a stressful situation?

4. Have you ever worked for a boss or with a co-worker who contributed to a stressful work environment? What was it about that person that robbed you of your joy? What in your character makes it difficult for others to enjoy working alongside you?

5. Gary Clarke speaks of some people having a "bailout clause." When have you had an experience when there was strong pressure to quit? What in the spiritual walk helps you resist the desire to quit?

6. Gary says that "everything opens the door to the next thing." Do you believe this? What in your life leads you to see how "now" shapes "next"?

7. Gary talks about the influence Jesus' and Gary's earthly teachers had on him. Why is it essential that unless we view those in authority over us with respect we can't grow to our potential?

8. In our postmodern world, we tend to be soft on morals and fully engaged in getting our own way. How is the concept of the body of Christ a positive correction to either being self-centered or getting lost in the group?

9. What does it mean to "pursue God"? How does knowing God affect how you feel about yourself and how you plan your future?

10. What do you think your calling is? What have you seen in your life that leads you to believe this calling is beneficial for others in the kingdom?

Other Bible references for you to consider:

Isaiah 56:1–2
Hebrews 4:1–10
1 Peter 5:5–11
1 Corinthians 12:12–24

THE MYSTERY REVEALED

———

Here's what I say:
God of our Lord Jesus the Anointed, Father of Glory: *I call out to You on behalf of Your people.* Give them minds ready to receive wisdom and revelation so they will truly know You. Open the eyes of their hearts, *and let the light of Your truth flood in.* Shine Your light on the hope You are calling them to embrace. Reveal to them the glorious riches You are preparing as their inheritance. Let them see the full extent of Your power that is at work in those of us who believe, and may it be done according to Your might and power.

EPHESIANS 1:16-19

Words: Carlos Darby / Photography: Seth and Suzanna Willingham

Ephesians is a book that I visit regularly because, while I may not be able to get my head around everything being said, the sense of God's love, wisdom, and purpose is tangible. Irrespective of my personal circumstances, I am always inspired and challenged.

In the opening scripture, you can feel the passion and purpose in Paul's writing. When I read it, I am filled with the hope of the relationship that is mine in Christ Jesus. The scripture sums up the heart of this book, and my prayer for you and me is that not a day goes by that we don't get to know Jesus a little bit more, and that the truth of His gospel captures our hearts and keeps us on the road He's called us to.

Give Them Minds Ready to Receive Wisdom and Revelation So They Will Truly Know You

The opening scripture from Paul's letter to the Ephesians, while on house arrest in Rome, is to early believers who were living in a time of great cultural pressure. Living a Christ-centered life in Ephesus in those days was a huge challenge; it was a place of counter-kingdom-culture where greed, lust, and idolatry were rife. It was also a city that would be of huge importance in seeing the gospel enter into Asia.

In this prayer, we find that Paul is asking God to "give them minds ready to receive wisdom and revelation so they will truly know You."

It says in James that we should ask for wisdom; it's something we can receive as a gift. Wisdom is associated with the way in which we lead our lives. I think Paul was asking for wisdom so they would be careful not to be influenced and distracted by the culture around them—so they wouldn't miss the second part: revelation.

Revelation isn't human wisdom; it's hearing the voice of the Holy Spirit speak to you, straight from God. The point here is to show us that the soul, or our natural man, has to position itself in focusing on Jesus to receive His words to us. When you know the true God, nothing else is as attractive as following Him and His ways.

The focus at this point in the book of Ephesians was not on what they—the Christians—should do as a church; it was about what would draw them deeper to the relationship they had entered into.

Open the Eyes of Their Hearts, and Let the Light of Your Truth Flood In

The eyes are one of the entry points to our hearts. It says in Proverbs 4:23, *"Above all else*, watch over your heart; diligently guard it because from a sincere and pure heart come the good and noble things of life." If Paul is praying that the eyes of their hearts be opened, that means he knows they can be closed.

Think about how many times we go through the motions of life, not really appreciating and enjoying the inheritance we received from being in a relationship with Jesus. If our eyes are closed to the experience, so are our hearts.

This reminds me of the older brother in the story of the prodigal son (Luke 15:11–32) who said, "Listen, all these years I've worked hard for you. I've never disobeyed one of your orders. But how many times have you even given me a little goat to roast for a party with my friends? Not once! *This is not fair!"*

The father's response is a great reminder for how seemingly blind and unappreciative we can be: "My son, you are always with me, and all I have is yours. Isn't it right to join in the celebration and be happy? This is your brother we're talking about. He was dead and is alive again; he was lost and is found again!"

The older brother's eyes were closed to what he already had. Instead, his focus was on his father's actions, his brother's transgressions, and on doing what was right so he would receive his inheritance.

We'll be waiting a long time if we expect our good works to produce life, to receive the intimacy we desire with our heavenly Father. Intimacy isn't earned—it's a gift! Guard your heart from the belief that you can't enjoy your inheritance today. See what you have already received because of Jesus. This will open your heart and will allow the ever-present and willing light of truth, which is the good news, to flood in.

We're light bearers, not light creators—we have to allow His light to come through and fill us up so that we can reflect this good news to our world.

"Guard your heart from the belief that you can't enjoy your inheritance today. See what you have already received because of Jesus."

Shine Your Light on the Hope You Are Calling Them to Embrace

This shows the importance of praying for revelation not only to receive something, but also to show us what we already have—like shining a light on something to reveal what it really looks like.

The word *embrace* is an important word in the scripture, because it's described as both "an act of holding someone closely in one's arms," and to "accept (belief, theory, or change) willingly and enthusiastically."

Jesus is personal. He wants to be embraced by your beliefs and attitudes toward Him. If we have a warped or misinformed perception of Him, we'll be pushing Him away instead of naturally embracing Him. With the cultural pressures

> "We'll never see the behavior until we know of our Father's acceptance through a relationship with Jesus."

and values that are constantly being promoted, the importance of what we embrace is crucial.

It's been said that what we embrace, we empower. We therefore have to embrace the good news—that Jesus made a way to enter into a relationship with Him. That's our promise and hope if we fully accept the finished work of Jesus on the cross and embrace the inheritance we receive.

Reveal to Them the Glorious Riches You Are Preparing as Their Inheritance

The glorious riches aren't just to be enjoyed when we go to heaven; we don't just enjoy Jesus in heaven—we enjoy Him today. God isn't going to die and leave an inheritance to us. The inheritance is what we get when we enter into a relationship with our God.

Yes, going to heaven is *part* of the inheritance, but it's only a stage in the journey of receiving it. Again, if we look at the story of the prodigal son, we see that we have complete access to our Father and His riches, which is Jesus. But we can sometimes focus on what we get *from* Him, more than the true riches of getting more *of* Jesus.

No matter what we go through in life, if we know the One we have given our life to, circumstances will draw us closer, make us wiser, and increase our gratitude to the One who took us through.

Paul, in writing to the Colossians, said, "He decided to make known to them His blessing to the nations; the glorious riches of this mystery is the indwelling of the Anointed in you! The very hope of glory" (Col. 1:27).

The riches we receive when we enter into this relationship aren't always what we thought. Our lives won't instantly be easier, and we won't always get everything we ask our Father for. The true riches—the mystery revealed—are that we receive Jesus, He lives in us, and we get to experience Him daily.

Let Them See the Full Extent of Your Power That Is at Work in Those of Us Who Believe, and May It Be Done According to Your Might and Power

When we acknowledge our need to turn to Jesus and embrace the truth that we're sinners saved by grace, we receive His Spirit and enter into the family of God. Because God is passionate about spending each day with you and building a relationship, He knows we need to be continually fed by the relationship we've entered into through reading His Word, through prayer, and through being planted in a community of fellow believers. But the power that brings it all together isn't the words on a page, the thoughts that come out of our mouths, or the activities we participate in.

We all know people who can recite the Bible inside and out, pray for hours each day, and volunteer weekly at church—yet, they're mean and miserable. The power that makes the Bible transform our thinking, makes our prayers passionate and active, and allows us to serve humbly in church comes from the power of the gospel.

As Paul said in Romans 1:16, "For I am not *the least bit* embarrassed about the gospel. *I won't shy away from it*, because it is God's power to save every person who believes: first the Jew, and then the non-Jew."

This relationship won't have any power to grow and produce the fruit we want to see without a revelation of the gospel. Only the power of the gospel can keep the relationship growing stronger. Too often we allow guilt and condemnation to drive a wedge between us and God, when the truth is that His acceptance isn't based on our behavior but on what Jesus did for us on the cross.

Our perception of God looking down, distant and angry, waiting for us to make a mistake, dissolves as our view of Him as a completely accepting and loving God grows through reading His Word and praying.

Paul purposefully prays first about faith and then speaks to the Ephesians about works. Like our generation today, they wanted to know the *why* before the *what*. They wanted to know that they were cared about first, before they would follow the instructions given about being the church. We'll never see the behavior until we know of our Father's acceptance through a relationship with Jesus. We want to be known *first*. The great thing is that the Father's heart is first and foremost to have a relationship with us; from that experience, we'll naturally be the church we were called to be.

More Than Just Words

The longer we're Christians, we face a danger of becoming accustomed to the language associated with being a Christian—we forget the meaning. The good news can fade into nice words we repeat around other believers. We lose the excitement of when this was all still new to us, and we find ourselves caught up with the mundane have-tos of the Christian life.

But Jesus didn't save you to make you a better person, more disciplined, or less annoying to Him and to others. He came to have a relationship with you that captures your heart and mind.

We want to know and be known by our Creator. We were designed to live in constant connection with Him. He's not an absent father whose spiritual DNA is the head of the family but whose love is absent from our lives. He's ever present and wanting to be known personally, honestly. He wants to listen to you and be heard.

Don't misunderstand—this isn't a guilt trip to make you improve your relationship with Jesus. I'm not quizzing you on your Bible reading, whether you've been praying this week, or bringing any other condemnation that might be creeping into your thinking right now.

I don't know about you, but sometimes I need a head and heart check of how I am actually *thinking* and *feeling* about Jesus. Is He someone who inspires me, challenges me, and gives purpose to my life? Sometimes it's good to take stock of my thoughts: *Is this real to me, or am I just going through the motions of being a follower of Jesus? Am I really following Him or the lifestyle?*

A. W. Tozer says it brilliantly: "I want the presence of God Himself, or I don't want anything at all to do with religion...I want all that God has or I don't want anything." I think a bit of confrontation about our experience with Jesus is a good thing every now and then.

Checked Out? Then Check Back In

Jesus was and is the message of God. He is the Word that created everything and creates in us a new life. He died to bring this message of salvation. Grasping the message of Jesus and letting it live out through our lives is what it means to be a follower of Jesus. Knowing the why of Jesus, who He is, what He did, and how He did it changes everything. And not just in the New Testament—all throughout the Old Testament, God the Father points to His Son as the answer to the broken relationship, that He would die to give us the opportunity to enter into it again.

This should change the way you perceive Jesus. It should change the conversations you have with Him and the way you live your life. We get such a short period on earth—shouldn't we want more from Jesus than just a life that's comfortable, a lifestyle you can be proud of, and children who want the same?

Sometimes in order to go fast, we first need to slow down and take stock of the conversations with Jesus. Is His voice familiar or distant? Is there a two-way relationship or not? Are we participating in our faith because we want to or because we feel like we have to?

We've all heard religious messages that scare us to the point of anxiety at not being good enough to enter the kingdom of heaven. But fear won't ever produce the right results over the long haul. Sure, it may get someone to act differently for a period, but fear won't transform hearts. Only the good news will.

Jesus lives in us. He wants to be experienced. He's the mystery revealed.

Q&A
CARL LENTZ

———

Straight-talking pastor Carl Lentz leads a fast-growing church in the heart of New York City, where he confronts secular culture and encourages the church to "occupy all streets" for Christ. He gives all the credit to Jesus, but also surrounds himself with people who enable this call on his life to be outworked. Focusing on the ones he follows, the ones he serves with, and the ones he leads, we spoke to Pastor Carl about the importance of the people in all our worlds, and how they impact the way we experience Jesus.

Photography: Matthew Lowden

CD: Can you tell me about how you first encountered Jesus and why you decided to follow Him?

CL: I think I have a unique perspective because of the house I grew up in. My parents weren't religious as such, but they taught me about a relationship with Jesus. They walked in such a way that it wasn't "you have to do this," but "you get to do this." So they wouldn't force anyone to be a Christian. It wasn't, "I'm going to tell you," but "I'm going to show you."

For me, my journey following Jesus had a lot to do with me following my parents' example. One of the reasons why I stopped was because I didn't see too many people I liked. Jesus was great, but I didn't know a lot of Christians I respected. So it was a huge problem—a disconnect between the two.

My parents were so consistent in their example that as I got older, I started thinking, *Man, everything they did—how they parented me, the way they failed and got up, what they were passionate about in life—helped me make the link between "this is who Jesus is" and them.*

That was my journey growing up, and then I decided to do my own thing. At nineteen years old, I connected some of the dots and decided there was no other way I wanted to live.

CD: When did you decide to go from being around the things of God to being in the things of God?

CL: I got lucky because I knew the first thing I wanted to do was study the Bible, and that led me to Bible college, which led me to Australia, and that led me to Hillsong Church.

I remember being at college and never having a desire to do church ministry, but just being planted in the church. Pastor Brian Houston told me if you get planted in God's house, you'll flourish. This is my story, and to this day I've never stopped being planted.

As I've grown following Jesus, there have been different landscapes and horizons. I'm not a big fan of writing down a vision and having dreams and goals, but I'll keep following Jesus; and whatever Jesus has in mind, I'm happy with that. Even with my wife—everyone has an ideal who they want to marry, and that's great—but I got a wife I never could have dreamed of.

When you follow Jesus, He'll take you a lot further and things will be a lot brighter.

CD: Do you think some people try to open doors that aren't meant to be opened? Do you think they need to wait for God and be planted for those opportunities?

CL: I think there's a spectrum, and we tend to sit in the middle of it. On one side, there's the idea of staying planted and wholly trusting God and not making one move—God will do it. I don't agree with that.

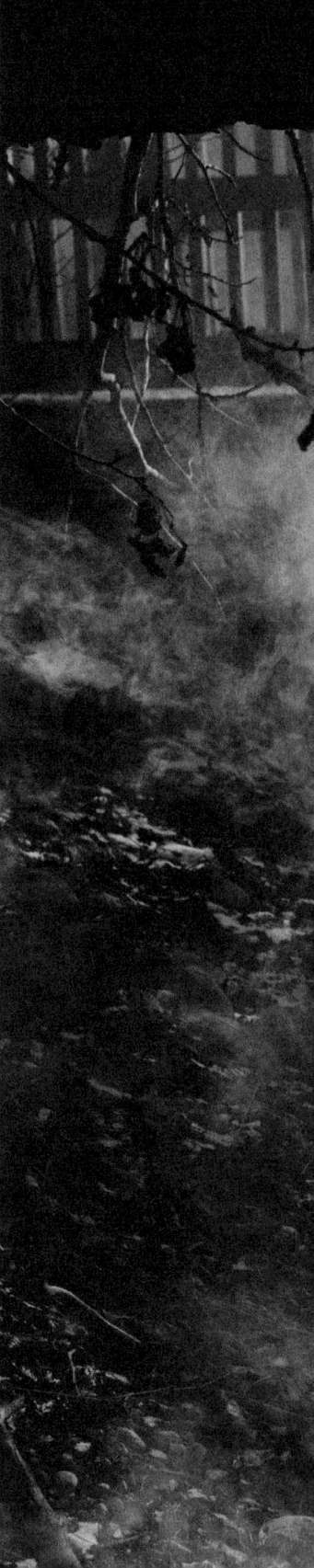

"We teach that prosperity is walking with Jesus— period. I think we've got to teach people about the middle ground."

The other side is saying, "This is my heart, and this is my dream; make it happen." I think that's weird too.

I think the truth is in the middle where you have to walk it out, you have to make decisions. If you have a dream, go. I believe the Holy Spirit will lead you.

Jesus always followed the Holy Spirit. Sometimes it was leading people on a boat, but sometimes it was leading people into death. We tend to forget that originally when people followed Jesus, they were following Him to death.

Someone's lifespan as a Christian back then was probably two months. So all this modern-day teaching on prosperity—follow Jesus and you'll get all this—wow! We don't teach and preach that in our church. We teach that prosperity is walking with Jesus—period. I think we've got to teach people about the middle ground.

CD: This is why it's so important to build this relationship with Jesus. You might know theology, you might be into the culture of church, you might even look a certain way, but if you don't follow Jesus, then what?

CL: If you trust the system, you can deal with shaky ground once in a while because you understand the anchor. I may not understand my season, but I understand my Savior, so I can walk through some pain, I can walk through some pleasure, I can walk through some shadowy seasons, I can walk through some spotlight seasons. That is trust. With Jesus, you can do it.

That is also where we find a disconnect. So many people don't know Jesus the person. They don't walk with Him, so they never get their footing because they're still trying to figure it all out. That's why this book is so important. That's why this topic matters. That's why I never talk to people about church. I always talk to them about *Jesus*. I don't want to get you involved in Hillsong New York City; I want you to get involved with Jesus. Once you get involved with

Him, you'll build His church. You'll be fine anywhere; if you love Him, this is easy.

So we are skipping the biggest step ever, which is, do you know about Jesus?

CD: Fathers have such an important role in helping shape their kids' perspectives of their Father in heaven. How did your dad model a healthy relationship with the Father and being submitted to His authority?

CL: It was such an easy transition for me. The biggest void in our generation right now is fatherhood. The devil hates fathers. When I say, "Your Father loves you," for a huge portion of the church, their immediate connection is that their father is bad. The challenge for this generation is to redefine fatherhood.

For me, it was such a pleasure to grow up in the house I grew up in, because I loved my dad so much. He showed me Jesus through his faithfulness, in his love for my mom and me, and in his harsh—or what appeared to be harsh—discipline. I knew it was God disciplining me through that. My dad loved me. He disciplined me because he loved me. Seeing Jesus through them was easy. Some people don't know that, so we teach that.

CD: How did your mom impact your view of the role of women in the church?

CL: My mom was never a subservient, dainty woman. There are some things about church vernacular where it's become weird, like, "She's my rib." I don't get that. It seems demeaning. In their marriage, my mom's voice was just as strong; she was a strong leader in her own right.

CD: You're now a well-known and influential pastor. How do you find your life in terms of following Jesus at this current level and in this season?

CL: I think the more ground God gives you, the smaller you've got to keep it with Him. I think I have a tough time understanding people who are overtly arrogant or self-sufficient. The more my wife and I go on with our church and see the influence grow, the more it is laughable that we could have done this. It's all God's grace.

I feel I am going lower as the profile and influence of our church is getting higher. Am I still praying? Am I still walking with Jesus? Simple stuff like that. Some things never change. We start walking with Jesus, and then we take a detour and don't walk with Him as much. I've got to make sure I'm walking, not visiting. This is residential living, not a vacation.

CD: You travel the world and meet all kinds of people, but how do you keep the sense of wonder?

CL: I've learned that sometimes it's not wondrous, it's not amazing. It's hard, and it's conflicting. It's heavy, but it's part of the journey. I think there's some wonder and awe in those moments, but by and large, I think being a Christian is putting your head down and obeying.

It's not my way of life to wake up every day and say, "Wow!" It's not my personality. Sometimes you have to push through the feelings. It's a reality. I think the word *experience* is a brilliant way of describing it.

When you experience Jesus, you're less consumed and concerned with the rest of the experiences that follow that. I can experience pain, I can experience pleasure, I can experience victory, I can experience loss, but I can handle all of that because I have experienced Jesus.

When people say, "I don't feel close to God," I say, "Who cares?" It's not about how you feel. If you feel good, you do what's right…sometimes. It doesn't always feel good to be faithful, but you do it anyway, and eventually the sense of wonder and awe comes from faithful service.

CD: I loved your message on occupying all streets. Tell us the heart of that message.

CL: It's about being the light of the world. We have somehow placed an emphasis on what you do and taken the emphasis off who you are, which makes people feel as if they're in a waiting game.

People say, "I'm a writer. One day I'll be a preacher," or "I'm a businessman. One day I'll get into ministry." I think that's deadly. It's not gospel. I loved the fact that that message was all about taking the ground you're standing on and not stopping to look at someone else's backyard and wishing you were there. Number one: it's not what you think it is. Number two: the ground you're on is holy ground, because you're there. "Occupy all streets"—the essence of it is our spin on the phrase Jesus said to people: "Go, be the Light of the World."

Wherever you are, be there. We're so fixated on the next chapter, we're not focused on the now chapter.

CD: What have you learned over the past few years about the people you serve and work with? How do you maintain yourself so you don't burn out?

CL: John 8:12: "Walk with me." I guess it's easy to walk with Jesus through the desert. There's no one else there. Then imagine walking through an amusement park filled with people. The landscapes change, the leader does not. For us, there's no difference. We just do what we've always done.

Jesus takes us by the hand into rooms with thousands—cool. It's the same Jesus when we're alone and in the wilderness. We're in the hands of the same God who took us through the last season. I don't use the term *burnt out*. A better phrase would be: when did you choose to *let go* of the hand of God? We should be able to handle the things that come into our lives.

I think the church can sometimes take the brunt of that. People say, "I'm burnt out" on church or on Jesus. It just doesn't make sense. We're doing something wrong; Jesus isn't failing us all of the sudden. I'm maintaining my walk every day. Making sure I'm in step with what God wants. The other stuff is neither here nor there.

CD: You do life with some people who are very influential in their chosen fields, but also actively following Jesus. What is it that has drawn you to have these people in your life?

CL: I want to be around people who are better than me at things. Some things people shy away from, I run toward. Insecurity gets you to surround yourself with people you're better than so you can feel better. For me, my mechanism is different. Everybody in my life is typically better at something than I am, so I'm always challenged and inspired. It's very hard to be complacent.

Pastor Judah has strength that I don't have. Instead of being afraid, I ask him how he does it. Show me your five friends, and I'll show you your five-year plan.

CD: Nobody is perfect, but we see some mistakes more than others. How can we be gracious and supportive of those alongside us, but also know when it's time to take a step back—or should we take a step back?

CL: It's wisdom. Galatians says to gently restore those who have fallen. The word *gently* can take on different forms. It's a tough one. We often say acceptance doesn't mean approval. Big deal. That means you can walk with people and challenge what they're doing. Acceptance doesn't mean you approve of someone's lifestyle. If we're friends, I love you and I accept you for who you are. I challenge you—I don't approve of what you're doing, maybe—but it's not going to be a deal-breaker. That way you can still walk with someone. I can't change you; all I can do is present my opinion on how you can change. Whether you do that or don't, it's on you. It's God's job to lead people to change and our job to walk with them.

CD: The volunteer teams at church give of their time, energy, and skills. Can you tell us about the servant's heart and what it does to a person's relationship with Jesus?

CL: The big advantage of serving is that you get to actively see the gospel at work. The gospel is meant to be given, and a lot of Christians don't give anything, so I think the gospel is dead in their lives. The church is an automatic way of being a part of the essence of the gospel, which is serving somebody else.

Why is our church awesome? Hundreds and hundreds—in some locations, thousands—doing their jobs and putting themselves second. If you don't have that, you'll never know what it is like to be a Christian.

CD: If I gave my life to Jesus right now, what would you say is my next step? What should I expect?

CL: The first thing I say to new Christians is: this can be anything you want it to be. If you want this to be a part of your life, it can be that. I always tell people the sky's the limit. I ask people, "What do you want to do? Do you want to be a distant Christian, or do you want to be a supernaturally led-by-the-Holy-Spirit kind of Christian?"

Most people say, "I want the whole thing." Do you devote yourself to it? You tell me what you're going to devote yourself to. Devote yourself to learning, serving, and leading, and you're all good. It's not a hard concept. There's no waiting game here. You don't need to spend two years reading the Bible to be effective—that's not gospel. You choose how deeply you want to be engrained in this.

CD: In your message, "Occupy All Streets," you say, "Who you are is not defined by what you do—it is defined by who Jesus is to you." How do you make that real to the generation you are leading?

CL: Jesus said, "Who do you say I am?" I'm constantly reminding people that who Jesus is doesn't change. How we see Him often does change, so your job is to see Him in the right way.

Is He your everything? Is He your God? If He is, then everything is going to be dictated by that. If you're doing a job you don't love, you're still very loved. What you do doesn't define who you are. It's a part of it, but is it reflective of whom you think Jesus is?

CD: How many problems would get sorted out if we just got our identity in Jesus?

CL: It's Matthew 6:33. Seek Him first and all the things people are chasing start chasing you.

CD: What is the consensus of non-Christians about Jesus and His church in your experience?

CL: There's a disconnect between what we say and what we do. It's hypocrisy. What's encouraging is that we can fix that. I'm excited about the future.

Twitter says, "Show your best, hide the rest." Sometimes, we live like that as Christians. We talk a great game, but the proof is not there. That's what we aim to correct.

You look in the mirror every day and make sure that person is doing what you set out to do. Don't worry about the people in the mirror you don't see. You don't have control of them; you do have control of you. If you're a mom, if you're in prison, if you're leading a company, make sure you're doing what God has called you to do. And the rest of the stuff will take care of itself. That's the gospel. Be light.

Carl Lentz

———

Carl Lentz is one of twelve Hillsong Church lead pastors globally. He pastors Hillsong New York, and has a passion to serve the city and make an impact worldwide. Carl and his wife, Laura, embrace a simple, dedicated faith in Jesus and are passionate about delivering the gospel in a method that makes sense to this generation.

Connect with Carl on IG @Carllentz

CONTEMPLATION

You observe my wanderings and my sleeping, *my waking and my dreaming,*
  and You know everything I do in more detail *than even I know.*
You know what I'm going to say *long before I say it.*
  It is true, Eternal One, that You know everything *and everyone.*
You have surrounded me *on every side*, behind me and before me,
  and You have placed Your hand *gently* on my *shoulder.*
It is the most amazing feeling to know *how deeply* You know me,
  Inside and out; the realization of it is so great that I cannot comprehend it.

PSALM 139:3–6

So *hear my final words*, my friends. Now that I have warned you about what's ahead, keep up your guard and don't let unprincipled people pull you away from the sure ground *of the truth* with their lies and misunderstandings. Instead, grow in grace and in the *true* knowledge of our Lord and Savior Jesus, the Anointed, to whom be glory, now and until the coming of the new age. Amen.

2 PETER 3:17–18

The amazing truth is that God has chosen us. His mercy is beyond anything we could dream. God has revealed Himself to us. He made His Word flesh in Jesus, and now we can experience the presence of God daily. There are those who try to steal our joy. But we can be assured that God is with us, and He will continue to walk with us.

Study the following questions and share your thoughts with friends.

1. What are the various ways in which God has revealed His truth and Himself to us? When have you experienced God speaking to you or giving you guidance?

2. How is Scripture unique from any other collection of truths? How closely does our Bible today represent the words God gave to believers in the original documents? What authority did the early church attribute to the Bible?

3. How do overly judgmental people affect your confidence in your relationship with God? How can you counter their influence?

4. What is the difference between a true follower of Jesus and someone who is only living the Christian lifestyle? When have you felt as if you were only going through the motions of being a believer?

5. Why is the transformation of a person into a follower of Jesus called the "mystery of Jesus revealed" in the believer's life? How is this different than self-reformation?

6. What is the difference between trusting God to bring about His will through us and striving to make our spiritual dream come true? When have you felt that you were trying to make things happen?

7. What do you think Carl Lentz means when he says that the walk of faith should be "residential, not a vacation"? When have you experienced someone visiting the faith? What are the characteristics of walking with Jesus?

8. Why is it dangerous to base your faith on your feelings? When have you been disappointed because you depended on your emotions?

9. How are you involved in serving at church and how has this impacted your life and those around you? What other opportunities are there for you to be involved in serving?

10. Carl says, "How we see Him often does change, so your job is to see Him in the right way." How have circumstances changed the way you've seen Jesus in the past? How has seeing Him correctly in the good and bad of life helped you through that season?

Other Bible references for you to consider:

Psalm 89:13–17
Romans 8:9–11
Psalm 37:3–6
Psalm 18:25–30

THANK YOU

To my wife, creative inspiration, in-house editor, and all-round amazing woman: Katie, I love you and am eternally grateful for all you are and your continuous support and encouragement to follow the dreams in my heart.

My two little girls, Maya and India, because my hope is that this book will help you on your journey in knowing Jesus personally.

To my father-in-law, Ray Newton, for all your legal work and personal investment in seeing this book come together.

To my pastors, Gary and Cathy Clarke, for your support and encouragement over the past decade. I wouldn't be doing this if you hadn't believed in me. Brian and Bobbie Houston, for their leadership and belief in the next generation, we truly are grateful for Hillsong Church—it's our home.

To a new friend, Scott Bakken, founder of Socality (socality.org), for always pushing me to dream bigger and introducing me to some amazing photographers. May this be the first of many projects we collaborate on.

Frank Couch for taking a risk with me and getting this book published; for making me laugh, being a mentor, and for the amazing contemplation questions you wrote.

Alee Anderson, my editor: you've supported me in so many ways. Thank you for making this an enjoyable journey.

To all the personal stories and interviewees who gave so much for the benefit of others, we're honored to share your story.

Graham Williams; for your wisdom, encouragement and getting this journey started. Thank you to all the photographers, stylists, makeup artists, and models involved. They all went over and beyond to help create the best possible images to illustrate the features.

Finally, to my parents, Simon and Lucy Darby, for supporting me, never making me feel like my dreams were ever going to stay just a dream, and my brother Louis, who is an inspiring person. I love you.

Abrupt Media

Our passion is to reach a visual generation by creating new resources that help people understand the truth of the gospel in a way that makes sense to them. We want people to have a life with Jesus that is experienced, attractive, and authentic. Ultimately, we want to be part of the church of Jesus being built one person at a time, seeing followers of Jesus being all they can be in Christ.

Connect with us at abrupt-media.com and on IG: AbruptMedia

CREDITS

Creative Director
Carlos Darby

Graphic Design
Emma Jackman (emmajackman.com)

Post-Production
Andreas Smitz (www.larssonsmitz.com)

Cover Image & Introduction: © Morgan Phillips Photography © 2013 and 2014

Title Page: Marlon du Toit **Back Cover:** Vlad Vasylkevych **Contemplation pages:** Hannah Radley-Bennett, Ed Peers (Chapter One); River Bennett, Blaine Nadeau, and Evan Michael Rummel (Chapter Two); Chelsea Crosby (Chapter Three); Evan Michael Rummel (Chapter Four); Hannah Burton, Andreas Smitz (Chapter Five); Vlad Vasylkevych (Chapter Six); Seth Willingham, Morgan Phillips, and Matthew Lowden (Chapter Seven). **Thank you & Credits:** Matthew Lowden **Final Thought:** Luke Williams

Models
Anne Kamping & Paul Knops (Visual story: The Rise and Fall / Location: Epping Forest, UK), Sheena Evans (Through His Eyes / Location: Camber Sands and Pett Level, East Sussex), Kaitlin Bliss (The Faith Adventure / Location: San Francisco, USA), Ruth Willmer & Kevin van Buerle (The Helper / Location: Albany, Australia), Kwabena Abboa-Offei (Faith of the Fatherless / Location: New York City, USA), Kevin Lei (Q&A Judah Smith / Location: New York City, USA), Pauline Smitz (Whose We Are / Location: London), Fadilia Bala & Miggy Del La Rosa (Q&A Charlotte Gambill / Location: London, UK), Alexandr Domanskiy, Iulliia Ivanova & Zhenya Lifshyts (Living from a Place of Rest / Location: Kiev), Esther Acheampong, Alexander Dushko, Tetiana Ravnushkina & Vova Kuharchuk (Q&A Gary Clarke / Location: Ukraine), Gregory Sczebel & Matthew Zoeteman (Q&A Carl Lentz / Location: Calgary, Canada)

Photographers
© Angel Abhayaratna, © River Bennett (thewolfpackmrs.com), © Hannah Burton 2014 (heburton.com), © Chelsea Crosby, © Marlon du Toit (marlondutoit.com), © Phil Edwards (philmedwards.com), © Matthew Lowden 2015 (mattlowden.ca) © Blaine Nadeau, © Ed Peers Photography (edpeers.com), © Morgan Phillips (morganphillipsphotography.com), © Hannah Radeley-Bennett, © Evan Michael Rummel (lookitsevan.co), © Kateryna Seleznova (katyaselezneva.com), © Andreas Smitz (smitz.co.uk), © Luke Williams, © Seth and Suzanna Willingham, © Vlad Vasylkevych (vasylkevych.com)

Editorial
Alee Anderson (aleeandersoneditorial.com), Maleah Bell, Derek Dugan, Shayla Eaton (curiousediting.com), Mike Potter, Alice Sullivan (alicesullivan.com)

FINAL THOUGHT

Paul says in 1 Corinthians 1:30, "Instead, credit God with your new situation: you are united with Jesus the Anointed. He is God's wisdom for us and more. He is our righteousness and holiness and redemption." The beauty of the salvation story is that on our own, none of us could ever *earn* the "new situation" we find ourselves in when we accept Jesus. He died and was raised to life again. If we believe in Him and His actions on our behalf we can enter into relationship with Him. God then sees us united with Jesus. He sees us perfect, not because of anything we've accomplished, but because of what Jesus did for us through the deep love He has for humanity.

We are righteous because of Jesus, but we are also a work in progress. God is the designer and is using the Holy Spirit to lead and mould us into our unique selves as a part of His body on earth.

"I am confident that the Creator, who has begun such a great work among you, will *not stop in mid-design but will* keep perfecting you until the day Jesus the Anointed, *our Liberating King, returns to redeem the world*." Philippians 1:6

We thank God that His love for us is all powerful and that nothing can separate us from His love. I pray that we live each day conscious of what it means to be a child of God united with Jesus. We have a new identity and can now walk through life experiencing Jesus in a way that is felt and known. We have been adopted into His household through the cross.

If you've never entered into a relationship with Jesus or if you have let go of His hand and wandered away from the relationship you once had, the good news is, all it takes is a single decision. You can say, "I need you, Jesus. I can't live this life without you and your absolute love for me. Please forgive me." The great thing is, He's not going to give it a second thought. He's already waiting for you with open arms. There's no guilt and condemnation for those who are in Christ, so He won't be holding your past against you. He wants to show you your new future that lies within a relationship with Him.

"He orchestrated this: the *Anointed* One, who had never experienced sin, became sin for us so that in Him we might embody the very righteousness of God." 2 Corinthians 5:21

THE † ONE

EXPERIENCE JESUS

"Every couple of days I'd pawn four to five hundred dollars' worth of stuff. Because of me, they no longer own any gold; I even sold my dad's wedding ring."

When I arrived to meet Steve D'Agrosa, he apologized in advance for being somewhat distracted by preparations for Friday Night Live, the weekly church hangout. His distraction betrayed the passion he embodied and the commitment he dedicated to his church. He placed his phone to one side so he could give me his undivided attention and explained that in no uncertain terms was this always the case.

Steve's story begins in Queens, New York City, where he attended Catholic private schools throughout his childhood. Although it wasn't always openly expressed, he knew that he was loved by his family; however, things were very different at school.

"I was really overweight as a kid and I got picked on and bullied because of it,"

CHAPTER THREE: THE ONE

THE
HELPER

Words: Carlos Darby
Photography: Chelsea Crosby

COLLABORATION

Abrupt Media and Noble Union

TAKE THE EXPERIENCE FURTHER

Find out more and watch the video at
theoneexperiencejesus.com

His divine power has given us everything we need to experience life and to reflect God's true nature through the knowledge of the One who called us by His glory and virtue.

2 PETER 1:3